First of an ongoing series *the babel anthology + french collection* brings previously untranslated writing from France to the Anglo world, along with new translations of little-known French classics. Alongside the clever French stuff a round-up of new writing in English from younger or less-recognised authors.

Short stories, travel, 'fieldwork' and poetry, sounds, voices and thoughts of the contemporary world, at *the farmer's market of the mind.*

fv Richad principn of Oxford Arts

the babel anthology

+ french collection

edited by Ray Keenoy

Ray Keey

Oxford

AIRSTRIP ONE

BOULEVARD

the babel anthology +

french collection

©Boulevard Books 2013

for rights in translated pieces:

see rights page

First Published 2013

Boulevard Books

71 Lytton Road

Oxford OX4 3NY, UK

Tel 01865 712931

info@babelguides.co.uk

babelguides.co.uk

thebabelanthology.com

ISBN13: 9781899460663

Boulevard Books are distributed in the UK & Europe by

Gazelle Book Services Limited, White Cross Mills, High Town, Lancaster. LA1 4XS.

Tel:+44(0)152468765

Fax: +44(0)152463232

email: sales@gazellebooks.co.uk

and available from Gardners

Typeset by Studio Europa

Printed and bound by

PRINTDOMAIN Rotherham S63 0QZ

contents

acknowledgements

Dennis Harrison, proprietor and *animateur* at the Albion Beatnik Bookstore in Jericho, Oxford, our world favourite bookshop and place for tea and literary and musical events of all kinds. It's also an incubator for hatching new writing – two of the pieces here were first tried out at the Phoenix Writing Group (bit.ly/VAOpYg) which meets at the Albion – and a networking node for various literary, musical and social groups and individuals, thanks to Dennis' faultless hospitality, generosity and effort.

Neil Anderson of Oxford Arts Meetup for encouragement and help with contributors and events.

Annie Rose for designing and assembling *tba* logo.

Graham Swift for the cover image taken from his beauteous *Flight of the Seagull*, copies (and other work) on sale at gfsmith.net.

Translators C.J. Young, Calypso Blaj, Tara Isabella Burton, Sara Helen Binney, Sophie Jones, Merryn Williams, Jennifer Tennant and Valerie Stylaniou-Worth.

Editors Ray Keenoy, C.J. Young, Tara Isabella Burton and Sylvain Atiocha for the French Collection.

All of our authors.

rights page

Boulevard thanks the following publishers for permission to use extracts from the books listed:

Huxley Scientific Press, Sundial House, 35 Marston Street, Oxford OX4 1JU+44 (0)1865 241073 sophie@euclidean.co.uk *FOR*

Heathcote Williams 'All bikes are weapons' from *Forbidden Fruit* 2011

Éditions Allia, 16, rue Charlemagne 75004 Paris

T +33 (0)1 42 72 77 25 allia@editions-allia.com *FOR*

Pauline Klein *Alice Kahn* 2010

Jean-Jacques Bonvin *Ballast* 2011

Éditions Attila, 16, rue Charlemagne 75004 Paris

téléphone/fax : 01 48 87 67 07 mail info@editions-attila.net *FOR*

Fabienne Yvert *papa part maman ment mémé meurt* 2011

Jacques Abeille *Les jardins statuaires* 2010

Bérengère Cournut *Schasslamitt: et autres contes palpitants* 2012

Éditions Maison de la Presse 'Les Vaches Noires' 63 Rue des Bains, 14510 Houlgate 02 31 24 10 19 *FOR*

Bertrand Guilbert *L'Amour en équilibre* 2011

ray keenoy

The babel anthology is a 'live' anthology, rounding up new and less well-known voices writing in English today and, with each volume, showcasing a different world literature.

First in the series *tba + french collection* brings new and previously untranslated writing from France to the Anglo world, along with some new translations of French classics. Alongside the foreign bodies we have a round-up of new writing in English from younger or less-recognised authors working outside the literary circles of hell of conglomerate publishing and celebrity namestering.

We include novel extracts, short stories, travel pieces, essays and poetry and work that fades in and out of different genres, gathering the sounds, voices and thoughts of the contemporary world into 'the farmer's market of the mind'.

Many of the authors and translators here are Oxford-based as we followed the 'think global act local' philosophy and started up using resources that were at hand. However this should not be mistaken for an internal Oxford project; we are open to writers, translators and editors from anywhere, please see the 'submissions' and 'next issues' sections at the end of the book.

the ghost of sani abacha

chuma nkwolo

"It was just a brief grab, you understand... And the way I figured it, I was owing Dabo Shogunle a few thousand naira that I could not pay, so I was dead already. Every three or so weeks a Dabo debtor was found in the gutters of Animashaun Street... I did not see that the black-suits downstairs could punish much worse than Dabo's boys. So I figured: grab her arse and die and go to Heaven."

This is the funniest, darkest story from Chuma's collection of the same title. We also highly rate his *Diary of A Dead African*.

Is this it? I asked the French Ambassador and he gaped at me through half-inch-thick glasses. He was clearly about to say something diplomatic and quite beside the point so I turned away from him and walked out, looking for someone without that Gimme-Contract glaze to the eyes. That was how I saw you. You stuck out in that party of ministers and hangers-on, with your necktie gathering your oversized collar behind its knot like a noose securing a sack of beans. You looked quite the objective journalist. Not that put out by my billowing bedspread. Hungry all right, but not the brown envelope type of reporter. There was something reticent about the cunning in your eyes. You seemed the type that won't print everything you overhear today in tomorrow's edition – perhaps because you were saving the really salacious stuff for your book. But I really don't give a damn when – or what – you print, you understand? If I can just get a straight answer to my bloody question: Is this it?

Take away five years and I'm standing in this cursed hall, a waiter. You wouldn't believe it, would you? To see me now – or to read my CV. That was the PR company, airbrushing out the bits that didn't sit well with the profile of senate president. Take five years and three days away and I was getting the slap that changed my life. I can still feel its sting all right, on this right cheek. Never saw a southpaw slapper before. Never saw one since, either. She was easily the most beautiful woman in this hall that night, and she had just received a bribe that she was keen to salt away in her suite up on the twenty-first floor.

I was the waiter serving her table and she had me carry the bag.

It wasn't one of those outsized *Ghana-mus'-go* bags. The bribe was in dollars you see, so the bag, though the weight of a rural health centre, (or six days' ministerial shopping at Harrods) was just a little bigger than an overnight bag. I hauled it and followed her towards the elevator. It was sixty metres away from the table where her American briber from the Button company simpered into his goblet of rosé. I had seen the flash of currency when she inspected the bag, as I sauced her peppered breast of chicken. I could have retired on that bag on my shoulder, but I was not tempted in the least. She was the wife of the minister for oil and steel, you see, and had arrived in a convoy of black limousines. Her black-suited protectors were just a scream away. Her husband may have been as scrawny and as wattled as a cockerel, but her security detail was no impotent joke. All I hoped for was a tip.

Yet, that would not have been enough to save my life.

She slapped me in the elevator. The temptation of the money had been easy to overcome. Her body was a different thing altogether. Was it the stun of her perfume? Or the bewilderment provoked by her beauty? Was it the hunger in my stomach coalescing with a madness in my groin? Or was it the way she stood with her back to me – and the curious muscles with which she began to tremble her mounds between the eleventh and the sixteenth floors? That was curious, will you not admit? Any other minister's wife forced to stand with a minion in an elevator would stand shoulder-to-shoulder. She would not turn fully away, leaving her backside to the unprotected glare of a waiter. And emphatically, she would not agitate them so. So I grabbed at them.

It was just a brief grab, you understand. I was not altogether mad; not then. And the way I figured it, I was owing Dabo Shogunle a few thousand naira that I could not pay, so I was dead already. Every three or so weeks a Dabo debtor was found in the gutters of Animashaun Street. There was nothing the police could do about it. (Some of the dead were policemen anyway.) I did not see that the black-suits downstairs could punish much worse than Dabo's boys. So I figured: grab her arse and die and go to Heaven. That was win-win in my book. So I grabbed her briefly, and she turned around, and slapped me hard.

And then she turned her backside back to me again.

That was the puzzling thing, you understand. The turning of her backside back to me again between the sixteenth floor where she dispensed the slap and the twenty-first where the door sighed open and the more conditioned air chilled the sudden sweat beading my face. She stepped out and walked, eventfully, down the corridor without a word to me. So I had five seconds to decide, as the doors tensed: whether to leave her bag on the floor outside the elevator and try to escape with my life, or whether to... then the doors began to close and I jumped through, and followed her down the corridor.

That was how I changed my life. Had the doors given me another moment to think it through, I would have made the more rational decision, and possibly ended up in jail. As it was, that same night, I was bedding the wife of the minister for oil and steel. I was her toy-boy for quite a few years. And every now and again she still gives me a call, (although I am far too busy these days, and far friendlier with her husband, to *fully* resume our old shenanigans). I had more *balls* than her husband; that was what she said to me, that first night. More *balls* than the minister for *steel*. How do you like that?

That was the night I first asked myself this question. As I rolled off her, as I stood in that falling elevator, with shrunken balls and pockets swollen with more American dollars in tips than any bag-carrying waiter dared dream, I asked myself,

Is this it?

There was a rank odour under the expensive perfume anyway. And she gabbled and slobbered in the grip of orgiastic joys. And if I entered heaven at all, it was on the turntable of a revolving door. So I maybe I went to heaven, but I was in and out in three seconds flat, and here I was back in waiter's livery descending to my table-ten-to-twenty beat, where the American briber was waiting, bleary with rosé.

Is this all there was to it?

Her money was enough to pay off Shogunle, anyway. I resigned of course. They all said I was mad, but I resigned immediately. I'd sexed the wife of the minister for oil and steel, so I couldn't wait tables any more. Over the next week I ate every dish on the hotel's menu. As a waiter, I had served them all, on an empty stomach, from duck to rump of lamb, from buttered sprouts to salmon, swallowing frustrated gobbets of saliva as I drank down aromas and served the food to the diamond-ringed fingers of the rich. Now I resigned and returned night after night, dressing my raging appetite in a polyester suit, washing down double portions of the restaurant's dishes with goblets of wine. And after every dish, as I stared queasily at the plates of shattered bones and greasy cutlery (like the broken mangroves and slicked wastelands of the oil delta) I wondered, Is this really it?

I think I think too much. I should never have read philosophy in school. All that Kantian junk and Hobbesian hobblings acquired by mimeograph from libraries full of empty shelves. Forty years ago, a clutch of indifferent GCEs would have secured me a respectable berth in the managerial cadre of the Civil Service; but that's life for you – I had come out with a B.A. Philosophy and had been lucky to find a waiter's apron. And I was days away from a gutter on Animashaun Street before I was lucky enough to grab the butt of the right minister's wife.

I was a few dollars away from broke as well, when she sent her car for me again. I sent the stunned driver away. She probably thought, *What balls!* again. (Although it was actually my moral scrupling with the last levees of the matrimonial taboo. That; and the smell I couldn't get out of my nostrils. Still, she must have thought, *What balls!*)

So she came herself, and… well, it was not just the perfume and the dollars; you understand? She had the kind of face you had to look away from, to continue to say No to. I did not look away. Yet, as I came, again and again, in that twenty-first floor hotel room, that revolving door into heaven spun faster and faster, until the exercise barely relieved the fetor of my life. And I realised that the true heaven on earth was located on the twenty-*fifth* floor, in the presidential suite where I had occasionally served the late General Sani Abacha.

Let me tell you about the presidential suite. If I finally get to Heaven and it is not like the presidential suite, I am coming straight back down. You cannot walk fast in those rooms. Your eyes are caught by a hundred and twelve luxurious things. The air itself is heavy with luxury and you are wading through the most sumptuous atmosphere, like a man wades through water… In my waiter days, when I knelt to set down the champagne buckets with which the damsels bathed the general (each rare champagne, the weight of a hundred thousand meningitis vaccines), once my knees touched that carpet, they did not want to rise again. Now, can you imagine *lying* on those beds?

But you can only imagine it, of course. In this country, money can only take you so far. After that, you need *power*. The general, Sani Abacha died here, you know, I saw this for myself. You should not believe the official line about him dying at home in Aso Rock. You see, it was passé for a dictator-president to die in a hotel room, however grand, so we bundled him up in a Persian rug, stashed him in the boot of a Peugeot 504 (to throw you journalists off the scent), and smuggled him back into his bed in the presidential residence. Since then, you cannot book this suite unless you are a foreign head of state – or a *very*, very senior member of government. And every time I dropped down the elevator, I remembered how the true heaven on earth can only be found on that twenty-fifth floor, in that presidential suite. Slowly, that became my obsession: to *enter* that heaven.

You see how simple it was? That seed of my ambition? I had never before thought myself a politician. But one night I was sitting there in the aftermath, smiling through cigarette smoke and thinking, *what a smell!* She was businesslike as usual, post-sex; bridling at the thought of habitually laying a layabout. So what do you want to do with yourself? she asked.

I was thinking of politics, I replied.

It was not hers to give, but her husband was minister for oil and steel, and probably the second biggest shot in the party. The diabolic incongruities of matrimony were adumbrated in this farce: that in due course he leaned, in my behalf, on the freshman candidate for the House of Representatives in Asata East, who withdrew for family reasons. I took over his nomination. It was a one-issue campaign: they wanted a water reservoir. I promised it. I won.

Of course every other candidate had promised it as well, but my own election was a matter of course – I was the candidate of the government party, which usually won every election. Even if I grew horns and a goatee, and bleated through my campaign speeches – like most of my fellow party candidates – my election was guaranteed.

I proved a natural, too. I went further and faster than those that had been at this all their lives. I think it was the way I said the first thing that came to my mind. I did not have a Sycophancy Filter, and they had never seen that sort of thing before: a politician that said the first thing that came to his mind. Yet, the contractors feared my lip and I was always the first to be settled. But because I talked the talk, my constituency loved me – at first.

That first year was great. We were the most productive Assembly in recent memory, passing three Acts within the first few weeks of session. (Our first Act was an anti-corruption law to insulate us from temptation: we doubled our wages, becoming the best paid legislators in the world.) After that we somewhat ran out of steam – till Ghana-mus'-

go bags began to arrive in our chalets. Energised, we pushed through the Privatisation Act that transferred a few national universities to the private sector. I bought a Grand Cherokee, which I drove discreetly in the small hours. It was a fine car, but... (look, a conscience is a terrible thing. Could never forget those years of studying mimeographs on Nkrumah's philosophy in empty university libraries... so) I drove around in my Grand-*one-million-library-books*-Cherokee, asking myself,

Is this it?

I slugged away at the job, and the currency bags continued to arrive. There was a whooping cough epidemic, children dying in thousands from fake vaccines. I got myself appointed to the Probe Committee (a coup, considering the competition). We approved federal budgets, retaining our share of the appropriation at the legislators' quarters. I built my Abuja mansion. The swimming pool was to die for – though I never swam it. Felt like I was swimming in Asata's water reservoir, it did. There's also an alabaster cupid in my garden, a placatory water feature gifted by the vaccine supplier whom I had drilled mercilessly on the Whooping Cough Committee. By day, the pissing of that white statue was all there was to hear in my quiet garden, but at night my house became a Babel, with all that coughing and whooping from the statue in the garden. Back then, it was a relief to get a call from the wife of the minister.

Unfortunately, by the time the general elections came around again Asata was still lacking a water reservoir. Of course, the government party had no problem 're-electing' unpopular candidates, but I was a man of principle. Besides, I didn't like being stoned at rallies. And, in any case, I had not started this journey just to end up in a mansion where I couldn't even get a good night's sleep. I had to focus on the heaven on the twenty-fifth floor – and an ordinary Rep could not presume to book the presidential suite.

I had to find another constituency and move upstairs into the Senate, and land myself the chairmanship of a big committee. Our minister had retained his portfolio, and his wife, her attraction to me. Yet, I was now wining and dining with her husband, and... well, I am a man of conscience, but she brushed aside my compunctions contemptuously. 'Just leave that matter! Do you know how a professor of history like him became minister for *oil and steel*?' I thought it was more polite to shake my head, 'I see! Do you know why he is still minister even though a whole *Nigeria* has been importing petrol for more than ten years? Look, this is a government by *kongo*. The day I stop sharing my own is the day he starts looking for another job!'

So, one night, through cigar smoke, I discussed my political future. I had just reached the minimum age for the Senate. In due course, I became the youngest senator in the Federal Republic. I was still in the middle of the electoral euphoria, when the bonus prize dropped into my lap. I did not even have to lobby for it. It was the outworking of an inexorable Political Horse-trading Formula made in Heaven to take me there. I am not much of a mathematician, but it works like this:

$$Power\ k\ negotiation = \{6\ GZ\ (Z1 + P)\ (Z2 + VP)\ (Z3 + S)\ (Z4 + DS)\ (Z5 + SP)\ (Z6 + DSP)\} / Nigeria$$

In plain English, the major political offices were allotted on the basis of Nigeria's six geo-political zones. Zone one had provided the president, zone two the vice president, zone three the speaker, and so forth... therefore my zone six was entitled to produce the senate president.

There are five other states in my zone, all of which had previously produced a principal officer. It was my state's turn at the trough. Now, there were only two senators from my state and the senior senator (a pregnant professor of economics on her third term in the House) was so clearly the right choice that she went prematurely into labour at the excitement of her prospective selection. Her supporters were in an uproar in the floor of the senate, but she was having her baby abroad (for the citizenship, you understand) and the other senators couldn't wait, so they gave it to me.

This victory party was a week in the planning, but the very first thing I booked was my presidential suite. I gave hard thought to the issue of heaven on earth and contacted the agency that supplied Sani Abacha's foreign prostitutes. They had a glossy brochure, but three days passed and I could not even settle on a shortlist of a dozen girls, so I left the choice to them. I wanted Orientals, Europeans, Latinos – the works... but I drew the line at Indian girls. I am superstitious that way. They had been the death of Sani Abacha, and my own session in heaven was not going to send me to an early grave.

I am the guest of honour, but I took my time to come downstairs. This is the meaning of power: the ability to keep hundreds of important people waiting on your whim. The dead general was a dab hand at it. It was the thought of these waiting minions that excited me most, as I rode those foreign prostitutes. Once again, the thoughts of windowless, teacherless classrooms, waterless taps and powerless electric cables attempted to torment me; but in this room, in this heaven, I am suddenly possessed by a begoggled demon, I am ridden by Abacha, and suddenly, it is Nigeria herself, the spoils of a war of military conquest, waiting for my thrust. Yes, the sumptuousness of this hotel is an ache in the wound. Yes, this oasis of plenty, rolled out like a mat in four directions, will electrify factories, water abattoirs, clothe pupils… so what? Jungles have lions and jungles have deer, and I would rather be senate president than slave.

The foreign prostitutes were worth their flight expenses. I climbed from climax to climax until, at last, I was past the seventh heaven. Then I rose from the last of those ravished imperialists. I, illiterate soldier, begoggled idiot, have done what the Awolowos and the Azikiwes could not do. I have conquered them all from America to rampant Spain, from France to broken Britain. They lay vanquished upon my carpets, on my beds, on my couches. And I am standing, still, not like Abacha who was waterlooed between Viagra and quisling India.

And this is the thing about the presidential suite: the bedspreads here are even more luxurious than my lace *agbada*. I toga myself like a roman emperor and descend to my victory party. This is my moment. After five years of agonising, despite the wailing bashees of the babies on my conscience, I'd far rather be senate president than waiter. That leaves just one question agitating my mind. Waiter, give me that champagne glass. And you, that salmon cracker. Damn. There goes my toga. Now I look as ridiculous as a potbelly on a general. But, here's the question I have for you, hungry journalist,

Is this it then? Is this what it is all about?

Chuma's books *The Ghost of Sani Abacha* and *Diary of A Dead African* are available online or from the *Albion Beatnik Bookstore* in Oxford. See also african-writing.com and blogs.african-writing.com.

in a thousand different cities

tara isabella burton

"I told the truth only once."

Burton's piece swaps between real life and life lived in the light of
ideas and obsessions in a way we find truly contemporary (even if
Knut Hamsun, Damon Runyon and D.H. Lawrence were already at it
before World War One.)

Why tell the truth? Nobody in Tbilisi knows my name. There is nobody to confirm my story, to determine my nationality, to correct my many-coloured account of myself.

When I am bored, I tell the henna-haired woman at the *chaikhana* that I am a famous English poet come to wander bare-legged in the mountain grass. I have hinted to my landlady that I have tapped telephones in Abkhazia. My butcher thinks I have a Georgian husband. My grocer believes I am French. Sometimes I have coffee with an obnoxious English journalist in an air-conditioned English bookshop off Rustaveli Avenue: he believes that I, like him, have come to sport a hideous panama hat and colonize this city one courtyard at a time. I am too clever to compete with him; he has carved out his own uncertain kingdom among the shattered glass and smoky streets of Perovskaya, where the strippers live.

I stay in the labyrinth of the old town, into which I have wandered like a princess in a fairy-tale and from which I can never escape.

I could not go if I wanted to. The streets double back on themselves; gardens divert themselves into courtyards; alleyways go blind. Maps are useless in this part of the city; I have learned long since to follow the stray cats instead. I don't know street-names. Instead I find my bearings by wrought-iron mermaids and stone maenads and sightless gargoyles that stare down at me from the tops of windows.

I have named them all.

It is easy to tell lies here. I speak Russian to Georgians and French to Russians and English to the Dutch. Restaurants and *chaikhanas* open and close with terrifying urgency; two weeks ago they built a glass casino over the iconographer's house. They've opened a cocktail bar on the riverbank. My name and history change with them.

I told the truth only once.

It was Holy Week. I did not believe in God.

The city choked on its stillness; the streets smelled like incense and bitter herbs. I had been fasting for almost forty days; fasting made me feel like I belonged. That God did not exist was immaterial.

That March I had decided that I would not be an Orientalist, not a spy, nor an anachronistic explorer nor one of the washed-up aid-workers relishing cheap beer in slimy basements near the Philharmonic Hall. I would be a spiritual exile. It was as good a reason as any to be here.

I remember Easter Sunday. I woke early and watched the sun rise from the old fortress; when the mist cleared the earth was new and I felt the thrill of possibility. Today I was Angelica, an Orthodox convert with a disapproving husband whom I had left behind in Lincolnshire As Angelica I fastened the scarf around my neck; as Angelica my skirts trailed into the dust.

I went to Sioni Cathedral because it was far from my apartment and nobody could recognize me there. The men did not set their eyes on me, they did not grope me as they had done when I first arrived. Angelica was a respectable woman.

The women gossiped in the courtyard; the queue to buy candles extended almost to the river. I positioned myself near the back.

I pretended the chanting made me feel closer to God.

I did what Angelica would do. I genuflected; I gesticulated. When the other women threw themselves to the floor, prostrate before the empty-eyed, gold-flecked face of Christ, I imitated them. I pressed my forehead to the floor. I tried to weep.

I didn't feel anything, of course – but then again I never did.

I saw him then.

He was broad-shouldered and dark-eyed; he looked like any one of the men who played backgammon after midnight on my street. He'd halted at the threshold; the dust-filled light from the dome flooded over him; his eyes were red and filth-streaked and there was nothing picturesque about his ugliness. He cried without fear.

I told myself stories about him: he was a returning exile, a refugee from Abkhazia, a poet who spent summers reading Lermontov holed up in one of the Svan towers I had never dared see in person. I told myself that I was Angelica, who would spend the summer reading the Greek fathers at a monastery in Kakheti.

When he caught my eye, my stories collapsed upon themselves. He pressed his hands against the stone columns as if to break them down; I felt the weight of his gaze press me to the floor. He saw me – he was looking beyond me – I don't know. He kissed the wall and did not vary his stare. He wept and his tears ran down the stone like candle-wax.

For the first time I felt shame.

I watched him as he visited each of the icons in turn, as he pressed his lips against them, how he smeared his tears upon them. I watched him as he placed his feeble candle among so many tiny others on the candelabra and pressed his forehead to the floor before the altar. I watched him sob as I had never sobbed in public.

I wanted to speak to him, to reach out, to catch his sleeve and beg him to allow me entrance to his private history. I wanted to memorize what he said and use it in some other context, collapsed and reformulated, so that next time, *next time*, I could tell my story with his voice. I could take him into myself, subsume his mortality into my own, transubstantiate myself into something solid, fleshly, real.

To speak to him required an introduction. I shuffled through my litany of identities, through my catalogue of identities. I exorcised them all.

I gave up and let him go.

There would be more cities. I would press eastwards against the frontier of my own consciousness, seeking someplace uninhabited by stories I did not know how to tell. I would take the night-train to Baku, perhaps the ferry to Turkmenistan, pushing back the fatal moment another thousand miles. I would forget Tbilisi as I had forgotten the others, or else tell stories about my walks up and down the Fortress, the samovar at the chaikhana, the polyphonic chants and the postcard-views of the old town.

The service continued without him. We sang and I could not keep on key.

"Lord have mercy; Lord have mercy; Lord have mercy."

There is more of Tara's strange voyage at perpetual.pelerinage. blogspot.com including the tale of how she won the *Shiva Naipaul Prize* for 2012.

war

paul ekert

"Reality is walking through the darkness of night, with the wind blown rain in my face, and the stars in my eyes, and knowing, really knowing, just for a short microscopic moment, that I'm alive."

It's okay, this isn't about an actual war... or is it?

It was a war of attrition and I was winning. The enemy suffered loses without comment, power fading with every passing second. Soon they would perish.

And yet, even on the verge of overwhelming victory, I felt no thrill. No glory. I didn't enjoy war. It was a tool. A necessary evil, if indeed such a paradox can exist. A solution towards my enemies' destruction. Nothing more.

Nevertheless, there could only be one winner and on the verge of victory I, all conquering hero, could not help a smile as I looked set to survive yet another encounter with this vile opponent.

Just a little longer...

"Hey!"

The enemies' unexpected reinforcements approached and inwardly I groan. All I had needed was a few precious seconds to finish the job, to obliterate the pest.

"What are you doing in that sink?" The reinforcements ask walking up behind me and pulling out the plug. Efficient female fingers prise the much reduced and now thoroughly deformed piece of soap from my hand.

"Not another bar," the nurse looks from me to the soap, and then her eyes dance away towards the ever present security guard.

"I've only just put this one in here." She says. She wants to be angry, but she doesn't have the courage. Not near me.

She looks at my hands and compares them with prunes. Not true. Inside there was blood, not juice. I know, I've checked. I'd watched it squirt away from my flesh as frantic hands tried to stop the flow. Self-discovery held the only truths worth knowing.

With one hand on my back and the other on my wrinkled fists, she leads me back to the dormitory. I study her face on the way. It's all angles and protruding bones, and I wonder for a moment if she would look prettier without the smooth white skin that covers rosy red cheeks.

"I think that you are at war with reality," my psychiatrist says one cold afternoon. I'd heard her use that exact phrase in the staff canteen. It got a big laugh from the other Doctors, even the ones she wasn't flirting with.

I know. I was listening. I was watching.

But I like the idea of being constantly at war with something and consider it as an alternative to making my hands look like prunes. Or perhaps it's the other way round, perhaps reality is at war with itself and I'm the only one who's noticed. Perhaps I'm the only sane man left. Perhaps television is reality, everything preordained, everyone told what to say, what to wear, what to do. Just like life.

Or is it that the other way round?

In a car, looking through dirty windows at dimly lit streets, I try to tell the difference between this and TV, and reality.

Reality.

Reality is walking through the darkness of night, with the wind blown rain in my face, and the stars in my eyes, and knowing, really knowing, just for a short microscopic moment, that I'm alive.

But by the morning, the knowing has gone away.

"Does soap ever remind you of your mother?" My psychiatrist asks, taking notes and showing me splodges of ink on white paper. "Are you at war with your mother?"

"No. I'm at war with reality." I say and that makes her think. And then I remember that I've not spoken to anyone for years... Or possibly days. No, it must be years because she writes it down.

Perhaps it was a character on TV that hadn't spoken for days.

Or perhaps reality was on the blink again.

Without warning, the room tips sideways and becomes soft all round. My arms are wrapped across my chest and tied behind my back. My head is fuzzy and full of nothing.

Why?

I was talking, speaking for the first time in years, and then... Then I realised, my psychiatrist must be Reality. It was so obvious I hated myself for not seeing it before, for allowing Reality to make a fool of me for so long. And so I dragged Reality to the sink, filled it up and held her under. She wriggled and jumped, but this war of attrition was soon over. Psychiatrists, it would appear, do not have the staying power of soap.

When Reality had died, I dropped her to the floor and went in search of a nurse to show her my victory. Through her tears, I heard her call on Jesus to explain why I had done what I had done, but he choose not to give an opinion. And who can blame him.

Then it was voices, hard and angry.

And needles, sharp and expressionless.

And then cocooned. Dumped like bad meat in a padded cell.

Safe and warm.

It was the question about my mother that convinced me to kill reality. After all, only an enemy of mine wouldn't know I was an orphan. Or is it the man on TV who's an orphan? I never can remember. Perhaps I'm on the telly now. If so I'll just wait for the adverts and leave. I hope it's a food commercial, I'm starved. Or is it the man on the TV who's hungry?

Only time will tell.

Time, my mortal enemy.

Reality is dead.

Death to Time.

travel piece

alexander darby

"I made an incredibly stupid announcement:
'English people love drinking.'"

Darby's China-set traveller's tale is rawer and rarer than most and now
of course 'the Sleeping Giant' has awoken (yawn)...

Around halfway through a three month trip in China I headed into the countryside, looking for some vestiges of the older civilization that seemed so absent in the urban centres I had been in so far. I knew I was some way on the path to achieving this when I got onto a decrepit, slate coloured minibus at Wuhan-a city in Hubei province - bus station, heading south to the countryside. As soon as I sat down, a small child opposite me immediately burst into floods of tears. The surrounding adults thought this hysterical and told me not to worry in pidgin Mandarin, it was only because the child had never seen a foreigner before. He continued to cry for the whole bus journey and I felt guilt ridden for hours, as well as a tad smug that I was going to a place far-flung enough that I looked different enough to cause such a response.

After a few days trekking between small villages, I came to one called Da Likeng. Da Likeng was like all the other villages I had been through: it was stuck in time. Men spent their afternoons sat on the bridge in the centre of town, dressed in faded, dark blue Mao suits smoking pipes, chatting with each other when they pleased and keeping silent when they wanted to watch the water. Its cramped, densely packed streets wound in between wet, ancient wooden houses, built in the traditional Chinese style. The whole place had the stillness of an old way of life to it, and I felt a little as though I was trespassing. Children working the fields that surrounded the village would throw me curious glances whenever I walked past, but thankfully none cried again.

I was a little worried as to where I was going to spend the night. In the villages I had gone through before, I was lucky enough to find a bed in an old woman's house. It had been something of an ordeal; none of the villagers spoke Mandarin and I had to mime sleeping, eating and then paying before anyone stood. To my dismay, after rubbing by forefinger and thumb together to symbolize money, they had rapidly sprung into action and brimmed with false hospitality before finding me someone to stay with. At least this time I had a guide with me. Unfortunately, he spoke no Mandarin and the only communication we had managed to have was about his shooting Japanese in the war, which he had crudely mimed while beaming with national pride. He had also tried to charge me an exorbitant amount of money for a cigarette he had given me, which I had mistaken for a token of friendship.

As we walked into the village, my guide met an old woman and led me to her house, which to my delight turned out to be a guesthouse, complete even with a shower (albeit an outside one that didn't lock and looked out onto the chickens below). While showing me around the house, I bumped into several other metropolitan Chinese who to my considerable surprise asked me where I was from in fluent English. After I replied they seemed delighted and called all their friends up. They were shocked to hear that I was here by myself and promptly told me that a big celebration dinner was in order. They then ran off onto a bike tour that they had booked, assuring me that we would see each other tonight. I bade them goodbye and, exhausted from the hike, collapsed onto the bed in my room.

Dinner that evening was uproarious. We had it outside on the terrace, next to the shower. There were about twelve us, all seated in a circle around a great big wooden table that was laden with delicious regional dishes. About five minutes in, our hostess brought up a bottle of *baijiu* and one of *mijiu*. Baijiu is a sickly, pale, eighty percent proof Chinese liquor, ubiquitous throughout the country. I didn't know what the latter was and hoped I wouldn't have to drink it, since it looked distinctly like lighter fuel, but I was quickly reassured that it was home brew rice wine. I was soon to discover that they both tasted revolting.

The hostess left and, in response to someone's question, I made an incredibly stupid announcement: "English people love drinking." The table burst into laughter and there then began an age old process, firmly entrenched in the national culture, of drinking the foreigner under the table. Since it is too rude to refuse a toast in China, I had to drink every time someone toasted me. My hosts only toasted me individually so I ended up drinking ten shots to their one. Once we had finished both the bottles a few hours later, I thought that would be the end of it, but to my horror, Wuji (a young student who was starting at Manchester next year) then said that the evening couldn't possibly go on without any more alcohol. Despite my less than eloquent protests, he ordered up another bottle and the process continued until it was late at night and I was staggering. I thought I might throw up, or pass out, or both and so I announced that I was going to bed. Not so, chorused the whole table. A woman from Guangzhou on my left said that they had a *surprise* for me. "What?" I asked, fearing the worst. The peasant whose house it was then came upstairs, as if on call. He was carrying a huge rifle and a gleaming smile spread across his face as he looked at me.

"We're going snake hunting!" they all cried out.

I unfortunately remember very little of what happened from then on, but the gist of it was a fairly raucous midnight snake-hunting trip through the neighbouring countryside. I don't think we caught any snakes, which is hardly surprising given that it was pitch black and the hunting equipment included nothing more than an old rifle and torch.

I woke up the morning after this escapade with a roaring headache and to the sound of several of my new Chinese friends knocking on my door. They burst into giggles when I emerged, fairly raggedly, and with tongue in cheek asked me if I had had sweet dreams. Ignoring my abrupt reply, they politely told me that they were going cycling again, and asked me if I would like to come. I declined the offer and they bid their farewells. One of them turned just as she was going down the staircase that left my room and began to recite a goodbye poem. It was gorgeous. I couldn't make out a word of it, but I could hear the fall of the metre and the beautiful shape of the tones, merging together into a unique song unlike anything I had ever heard before.

trans-euro-night 1972

leon lukas

'...we were going deep into Germany, mile on mile.'

The train as time machine.

I'm travelling without a seat so I have to stand in that little space between carriages and balance like a ballerina, feet angled, bracing against the train running along. I'm wearing my blue sandals – I'm on holiday! – they're pressed against the dirty silver floor with raised lettering that says *Ferrovie dello Stato*, 'Railways of the State', but all worn down on one side. Now I drop my hand to the half-lowered window and the smooth rounded-off edge of the glass, special tough railway glass, makes a hard, comforting rim for my fingers to rest.

When this train took me through the gaping rail yard of Aachen, after the Channel, it was already evening, colours fading but even so I noticed a single green carriage standing on its own, buffered between long ranks of grey German Bundesbahn coaches. Like that, isolated, all on its own, like a grubby orphan dressed in a charity uniform, sent to the village school, getting mocked and despised... On its side the coach showed, just about, under the dust of endless frontier crossing, the letters 'P.K.P.'.

What does 'P.K.P.' stand for? Portuguese something?

Baffling.

Then it came – P is for for *Polski*! Polish State Railways, and then my train, the Trans-Euro-Night routing Oostende-Köln-Freiburg-Basel-Genoa, lurched and swayed from out of Aachen rail yard, picked up motion, quickly leaving the flatlands between here and Oostende-port. The map behind glass that was screwed on the carriage wall by the toilet showed that, after Aachen, we were going deep into Germany, mile on mile.

Germany! I lay the little knapsack that holds my book, my folding map, the sun cream and the purse of foreign money, down between my feet, keeping it upright pressed between my calves, and I stare out into the night rushing past, warm diesely air tickles my throat and hair. The train is running through Germany, I think of something in the old language, because this is where it came from, *Dus iz oykh geven amol amol der zayde's haym!* (This was grandfather's country too, once upon a time!). But he would never go back.

The train is cutting now through a night that's become so dark, deep and dark, it pushes on fast, never stops, past stations, platforms, sheds, junctions, fields, outbuildings. Even in the fleeting light I see Germany is tidy, tidy houses, neat bushes, cars in rows. It's tidier, it's neater than anywhere, anywhere at all.

And there was the Polish wagon, P.K.P., back in Aachen, when it was still light but fading, that made me think of something, something to push. I reach down to the knapsack, any chocolate left? A bit? The something comes back, I push as it comes, the something that begins little, grey, sad but can – if you're not very careful – fold out into a big swallowing darkness, darker than the dark out there. The more you keep it out, the more it bursts in, thief at the door, a burglar, a rapist.

The closed-up carriage, the P.K.P., it's Poland, it's running back to Poland.

Eyes closed I rest my hand against the damp window, feel for the hard rim, shivering in a thin shirt.

***

As a child in Hammersmith she'd buy rye bread and slices of Tilsiter cheese for her *zayde*, her grandfather, in an old-fashioned Polish delicatessen, a quiet shop, a temple of sausage, purple borsht in tall jars and a pale-skinned blonde who served behind the marble counter, with her face and neck so white they were marble too. The blonde would look across the marble at her and say *Zen Dobre*, 'hello' in Polish, she didn't know the language but Grandfather did. And now she thought, and now she thought – was that why he always sent me for the Tilsiter and the rye? Glossy, smelly cheese, spicy chewy bread? Zayde's little taste of *der alter heym*, 'the old country'.

But and but and but and here it crashes through, the dam bursts, a whole village swept away – you know – everybody drowns, the zaydes and the bubes, the babies, the dog and the cats, the rabbi the rabbi's wife called *rebbetzin* and the *kinderlekh* who were the kiddies in the photograph they won't be rabbis at all, and there was that other Poland that was behind the broken dam that flooded everything, the Poland in grainy black and white that unreels doesn't stop, images as dim and shadowy as racial memory. She barely struggles now to hold it, the train is crossing Germany, deeper and deeper into Germany!

As they slow down through a station well inside the Ruhrgebiet, in the dark mass of night-shapes, out there where there must be coal towns and steelyards, a sudden pool of fluorescent light and a young man's face in it, her age, waiting for the late train alone on the platform, a beer can in his hand. To get him home to the flat, where Papi and Mutti are snoring. Judith tilts the oval of her face at him, smiles through the glass, her brown eyes gaze into his blue ones for a second, inches away. He looks at the disappearing train open-mouthed, his lips shiny with the beer and he still sees the after-image of her face and her round eyes, brown eyes, beautiful eyes, a love he'll never touch…

Inside the train she stares out along the infinite sightlines night makes, the horizon so far off in the darkness and faintly edged by the greeny-yellow glow of the station light left behind. Why is the railway light here greeny-yellow? She feels too vague to understand. The grainy images flicker closer in. There is a special German lettering they use on all the signs. She starts to feel how cold and alone she is on the Trans-Euro-Night, there are hours and hours to go before landfall in the South, then there'll be a hot midday sun pouring itself down, down over the warm cities and friendly seas of Italian Liguria.

The Trans-Euro-Night halts at a signal out in open country. She smells the pine-trees then sees them, a big moon squatting in their top branches. Breathing the green pine-scent she detaches herself in mind from the metal floor, one sandal on the silvery 'dello' from 'Ferrovie dello Stato' and imagines herself running under the trees, the soft needles brushing her shoulders and making her leap like a startled animal, light glinting on her white legs and the moon caught up in her dark hair. The train jerks itself into a tunnel, closing everything in darkness and choking diesel.

She gasps, shudders, tries to concentrate on tracing her finger along the metal sign under the window, picking up light railway grease lying on the raised letters, 'nicht hinauslehnen/non sporgersi/ne pas se pencher en dehors'. She sighs, the mental barricade just collapses, she sees the cattle-wagons marked *P.K.P.*, *Chemins de Fer Français* or *Deutsches Reichsbahn*, people sealed up inside them, trains rumbling across tracks through Germany to the camps in Poland.

After the tunnel, Trans-Europ-Night races on across unlighted rails, deep into Germany but travelling South, kilometre on kilometre. Her pale face is held behind the glass. Pushing a hand down into the blue cotton knapsack lying between her feet, she touches her passport, its cover is stamped with yellow stars, the twelve yellow stars of Europe.

(From an unpublished collection of Europe-set stories).

night in the sahara

I. hodson

"Tiny amidst the ocean of deep night, an orange glow flickers."

Certain places seem to burn holes in peoples' minds and then they try to heal themselves by writing. Far better to stay at home!

Sometimes a vision remains in your frame of reference as though every part of you has been waiting for that precise moment to marshal itself into position, readying sight, sound, thought and sense to preserve a moment as though in the knowledge that it will one day be needed, will connect with all of the rest of your past experience to slot into place as though fulfilling a missing connection.

As you sit under the stars, try to think about all that has happened in that place, for millennia before you – and even then it will not be enough to glimpse an infinitesimal sliver of the magnitude that surrounds you. A darkness more black and more complete than anything you can imagine. There is something about that darkness. It is not threatening – it does not conjure up images of lurking intruders; animals circling slowly waiting for the fire to die down before approaching with a menace in their eye and slavering lips; nor does it terrorise with a nihilism of the spirit, no cackling glee at the nothingness that its black recalls.

But nor is it benign. It hints at the extremes of the universe, stretching as though beyond them. By day there extends an undulating sea, roiling mass of playful dunes specked by gnarled but happy shrubs inexplicably nourished. Far off, the dunes are unreal undulations, gleefully rolling with abandon, caring nothing for distance or habitation or boundaries, but spreading expansively like irresistible flood waters devouring the houses with a casual flowing of itself. Closer can be discerned that each dune, no matter whether the larger ones that hide all behind from view or the smaller ones that are barely more than piles of sand, has its own character, a meandering ridge of varying shape and trajectory leading to the valley in miniature below its brow, some bare and clean standing bold in confident parody of themselves, some with succulent branches or gravel spoiling their near-smooth surface, a simplicity unachieved. Some are bored through with the burrowed hollows of gerbils, some tickled by a trail along their surface of the gentle tracing of beetles, or of fox paws, hinting at an unseen kingdom below the superficial sand that blows away at the slightest whisper creating a shuddering caress over the more solid mounds beneath.

Yet by night this backdrop disappears. It is not that it is there but darker, subdued by the departed sun into slumbering while it awaits the dewy dawn. It has gone. It is as though a vast curtain of night has fallen heavily upon it, painted with a black so thorough that the memory of the dunes it conceals cannot break through but is instead swallowed into its voracious embrace.

Tiny amidst the ocean of deep night, an orange glow flickers. Though

the babel anthology

the dunes, too, have glowed orange, this does not echo that static luminosity or brooding warmth. The fire is of a different hue, more metallic somehow, more insistent yet ethereal, a unique colouring that only flame can reveal. The twigs and brush used to light it have been dragged from around the clearing, and the shrub gives off a distinctive aroma as it burns, the woody undertones finessed by a more herby smell that hints of spring, and fertility and life. The thick smoke playfully circles around, occasional gusts of wind causing it to change direction and to become suddenly cruel, curling its ash and debris into the eyes and mouth, a reminder that the wind and fire do not answer to those that tend it. All eyes are transfixed by the blaze, each branch as the fire takes hold now surging in a bright extravagance illuminating the circle of sitters as though delighting in its capacity to surprise, then dying down and joining the other embers – once shaped and distinctive, now one with the other vestiges of those that had been its neighbours on the branch in life, burning, returning to the sand from which they grew. The faces turned into the circle are warm, comfortable – the scene no different from a cosy parlour where the hearth provides the focus and those that have come in from the cold gather around it, heedless of all that is outside them. The light brings a strange community to the group. Those selected by the fire for illumination become an object of focus, a spectre outlined against the dark backdrop, before dropping into dusk once more as the playful flames seek another subject. A drum is brought out – simple, white with a red hand imprinted on its skin in primordial echo of countless other marks of man on objects that says 'I claim this'. The notes of the drum are dissonant with the singing, but the inexorable rhythm transcends all melody, and the sound punctures the surrounding silence with a triumph of the tangible within the ephemeral as it imprints its memory on the canvas that awaits reluctantly the insistence of activity upon it.

You stare at the stars. Or you turn away from the fire to look into the void and it is like standing on a precipice. The singing is loud, is carrying where light will not, and you realise that the fire's warmth reaches you but that the other way is a vastness that beckons. As you see the immensity unfolding before you, as the light becomes dimmer and you forget where you are, you forget *that* you are, because the singing surrounds you and you realise that it still resonates through the sand where the light cannot penetrate, and the sounds ruffle the wizened leaves of the shrubs like they have always done, like they have done since time began. And you are suspended in this space, this space where the only light comes from the stars, enveloped in a synergy of earth, sky and sound that transports you back to a time, millennia ago where songs were first sung, that has seen this before, and knows all. To you it is new, but you are on the sand, the desert holds you, and for this moment you are in the liminal space between worlds. As you travelled back to this prehistoric dreamtime, you shrank – in our normal life you are large, the world is there for you, and the troubles that you encounter fill the space around you. But in the Sahara at night the things that occupy you, no matter how large, can only extend pathetically, weakly, impotently to be insipidly swallowed up by the space, the air, till as you arrive that moment thousands and thousands of years ago you realise, in a single moment of epiphany as pointed, as contained, as that star that hovers smiling – you are of this earth. That is all. Nothing that you have brought with you into the desert matters, nothing that you think or trouble yourself with can matter here. You are admitted, but you must come alone. Yet this thought does not terrify, but comforts. It is a release.

The wind is growing stronger, curling into the clearing and insisting on admittance into the circle of light, the fire bending suddenly and licking the sand before leaping up and flaring as the gusts claim control.

***

Dawn. Dew tinges the ground. The sky glows rosy, the pinkish rays innocently proclaiming their presence as though the night has never been. Voices, camels, sand russet, stretching itself to the new sky. The dew is fresh.

the uninvited

(extract)

katie low

The Uninvited is a contemporary reimagining of Simone de Beauvoir's novel L'invitée (translated as She Came to Stay), a fictionalised account of how two women nearly ended her partnership with Jean Paul Sartre. When Isobel, bored in London, reads Beauvoir's work, she decides to model herself on its heroine and move to Paris. The story inspires her to pursue her former lover Chris and drive his demanding new girlfriend out of his life, just as on the last page of L'invitée the interloper Xavière is murdered...

(We have ben assured that no girlfriends were murdered in the creation of this piece – Ed.)

.

Suddenly the dull roar of the train changed pitch and they were in the tunnel. Staring into the blackness on the other side of the window, Isobel closed her eyes to block out the reflection staring back at her. She thought of Chris and his new woman and she wanted to cry.

"Sorry. I guess I haven't got much to say today. I'm a bit preoccupied, to be honest. There's this girl that I've met."

Isobel caught her breath. She had told herself that this conversation would happen one day, but she had never dared imagine how it would be.

"What's she like? What's going on?"

(*L'invitée began with a woman named Françoise staying up late to type out a playscript with her young friend Gerbert. Françoise watched him as he dozed off, asking herself what would happen if she said that she loved him. Then she stopped. There was no point in wondering how she felt, because there was someone far more important in her life: Pierre.*)

On that day in March Isobel had waited in the Metro at Sèvres-Babylone, feeling hot and clammy in spite of the cold weather. She had been about to pace to the other end of the passage when she saw a tall figure in an oversized grey overcoat approaching.

"Hi," she said, trying to keep her voice level, "good to see you."

"Hey there," said Chris, "sorry I'm late." He gave a tight smile. She put her arms out but realised he was going to kiss her lightly on both cheeks.

"How's it going?", he asked.

"Not too bad. You?"

"I'm fine," he said, "Anyway, what do you want to do?"

"Can we at least have coffee first?"

In a side street nearby, there was a small cafe, with little round tables and cane chairs pushed together in rows outside, like all Parisian cafes. They sat down.

"I was going to ask if you knew somewhere round here worth seeing," she said.

"Well, we're in Montparnasse. I think there's a cemetery that's quite famous."

Françoise was a writer working on a novel, although she never seemed close to finishing it. Pierre was her partner, a theatre director planning to stage the play that Françoise and Gerbert had typed. Françoise kept emphasising how much she and Pierre loved each other, how devoted they were, even though they often acted more like friends than lovers. They shared a bed but never had sex, and they talked freely about his affairs with other women. He said they were meaningless, and Françoise seemed truly not to care. It was easier to understand Pierre's sister Elisabeth, an artist. She chose to sleep with anyone she wanted to and was proud of it, but for most of the book she was unhappy because of her married lover Claude, who would never leave his wife.

As they walked, Chris looked straight ahead and Isobel watched him. His shoulders were sloping and his head was bowed; she suspected that the fact that they were on the move was his excuse for not talking to her. Turning into a quieter road, they passed a street sign: *Cimetière du Montparnasse, ½ km*. Chris glanced up at it.

"Sorry. I guess I haven't got much to say today. I'm a bit preoccupied, to be honest. There's this girl that I've met."

Isobel caught her breath. She had told herself that this conversation would happen one day, but she had never dared imagine how it would be.

"What's she like? What's going on?"

"She's nice, she's pretty. Well, she's nice when she wants to be. I don't know, sometimes it's fine, sometimes it's like she wants to behave as badly as possible just to see what I do."

Chris was confiding in her. Or maybe he just wanted to say all this aloud, and she happened to be there.

"Why do you let her do that? Doesn't what you want matter too?"

He shrugged. "Yes, but she's got me."

In the early chapters Françoise became friends with Xavière, a bored nineteen-year-old girl from Rouen. It wasn't clear how they had met, but Françoise soon introduced her to all the places in Montparnasse that she, Pierre and their friends frequented. Xavière was rather fey – charming one minute and sullen the next – and it was hard to see why Françoise was so considerate. Then, on the suggestion of Pierre, who hadn't yet met her, Françoise invited Xavière to come and live in Paris amongst them. So she came to stay and became l'invitée.

In the cemetery Isobel wanted to go and look at the plan marking the graves of famous people, but it felt as if Chris would leave if she deserted him even for a minute. They might as well take the path on the right. Not very far along was a group of Japanese tourists, posing in turn in front of a pale granite tomb while the others took pictures. She went to look.

JEAN PAUL SARTRE

1905-1980

SIMONE DE BEAUVOIR

1908-1986

"Hang on, this is a famous one. I'm going to take a photo."

Sometimes Xavière was sweet and charming, but more often she snubbed other people's efforts to be friendly. Moving into a bedsit in the cheap hotel where Françoise lived, she was not afraid to force her and Pierre to change their plans each day because of her. Most of the time Françoise seemed not to mind. Pierre was less patient at first, but soon he began to be fascinated by Xavière. It was hard to understand what he was thinking. He didn't want to sleep with her; it was more that he needed to be the most important person in her life and absorb all her attention. Xavière was still infuriating, but she seemed happy to play the role Pierre demanded of her.

The tourists had not yet finished. As Isobel waited, Chris took up their previous conversation.

"For example, last night, we went out. We were in a bar and finally, at about three, she wanted to go home. But then she started chatting to some guy there, so I just had to sit and talk to them both. I'm not sure if she really wanted to flirt, or whether she was just seeing what I'd do. Obviously I wasn't going to leave them alone together. Anyway, after a while he went off, but she wanted to carry on drinking. In the end I had to take her home." He paused. Isobel tried to stop herself wondering what had happened when they got back. "It's not fun any more."

"So why don't you just not see her, then, and tell her to stop doing that stuff?"

"I told you, I can't. There's something about her."

The Japanese left. Isobel noticed how the neat lines of grey monuments matched the cold sky. She lifted the camera and took a photograph, careful to include the ragged flowers scattered on the tomb but could barely keep her hands steady.

Françoise tried not to be upset, and Pierre kept saying that Xavière was no more significant than any of his other women. Then Françoise fell ill, and Pierre and Xavière came to visit her in hospital and told her of how they'd explored Paris together, and of the adventures they were all going to have when she got better. For a short time they became an inseparable trio. But then Françoise came to believe that she really was losing Pierre to Xavière, and there was nothing she could do about it.

"She'll probably want to go out again tonight."

Suddenly his blank expression enraged Isobel. "For God's sake," she snarled at him. "Don't think that I can't stop this. I won't let it happen."

Chris turned away with another shrug, but it was the dull realisation that he would not react with much interest to anything she said that stung her more. He muttered something.

"Sorry, what was that?"

"Come on, Isobel, you know that you can't say that kind of stuff any more. Just leave it. Please?"

They carried on walking, and made a whole circuit of the cemetery in silence. Back at the entrance again, Chris turned to her. "Look, I need to go. I really need to get some sleep. And to be honest I think it's probably a good idea anyway."

A perfunctory hug and he was gone. She stared after him. Soon, hunched against the cold with his hands still in his pockets he would walk into another cafe, but someone else would sit beside him.

At last, Xavière began to resent Pierre's attentions. She went out drinking with other people and didn't tell him. She flirted with Gerbert and then they had sex while Pierre, skulking outside, watched through the keyhole. Françoise talked over Xavière's behaviour with him, and loyally tried to reconcile them.

One night, as they sat in a bar together, Xavière took a lit cigarette and pressed the tip into her arm, not flinching, saying that it didn't hurt, as Françoise looked on in horror. Anyway, by then Xavière didn't care if what she did made Pierre jealous, and eventually he lost interest in her. At that point Françoise went on a walking holiday in the countryside with Gerbert. One night they slept together, and Françoise hoped that with him she might find a simpler kind of love alongside her relationship with Pierre. But this part of the story wasn't important. What mattered was that Xavière the interloper, the unwelcome guest, had been driven out. Françoise and Pierre were reunited.

Isobel went back along the road where they had been earlier. After a while she came up a narrow, sloping street somewhere in the fifth arrondissement and was confronted by the biggest bookshop she had ever seen, a huge building more like a department store, with its name branded in giant letters across five storeys of windows. She paused and shivered in the wind.

Inside, she was beginning to wonder if there was a section for English books when the name on half a shelf's worth of spines caught her eye. *Beauvoir*. For a second she wasn't sure why it seemed familiar, and then she remembered. She hadn't known that Simone de Beauvoir had written anything other than *The Second Sex*, but here were four or five novels, as well as volumes of autobiography. Isobel picked up each title, fingering smooth white covers and peering at the dense print inside. In the introduction to one, *L'invitée*, she read it was Beauvoir's first novel. The book was quite short and there was a stylised picture of a woman in a green dress on the front.

On the journey back to England, though, her purchase remained untouched: it was easier to sit and gaze at the darkening fields outside. Suddenly the dull roar of the train changed pitch and they were in the tunnel. Staring into the blackness on the other side of the window, Isobel closed her eyes to block out the reflection staring back at her. She thought of Chris and his new woman and she wanted to cry.

christiana, the anarchist colony

fleur kinson

"Who wants to gawp at a lawless lifestyle based on no greater aspirations than the freedom to get stoned, talk bollocks, and believe in hokey bullshit?"

Kinson, a *Sunday Times* travel pages regular, was converted to an earth-digging, freewheeling lifestyle by a visit to Christiana (sort of).

The Christianshavn district is neat and calm. Or it would be without today's howling wind and rain. It sprouts yellow ochre buildings and distinctive spires. One giant church-topper, boldly painted chocolate and gold, is shaped like a tall, thin helter-skelter. It powers high into the sky and seems to serve as a landmark for the whole district. Canals and tiny harbours riddle the streets, boats crammed into every crevice – a delirium of rigging, plump hulls, glossy wooden floors. I walk for miles, peering at buildings, watching the Copenhageners and trying to grasp their city. The rain veers capriciously from fine spit to aggressive, pounding drops. I have no umbrella, and try to shelter beneath a tattered paper map of the city.

At some point I say 'fuck it' and decide to go see Christiania, the famous hippie-anarchist colony that borders Christianshavn. Before this moment, I had zero interest in ever seeing the place in my life. Who wants to see a bunch of potheads living in squats splattered with graffiti? I had thought. Who wants to gawp at a lawless lifestyle based on no greater aspirations than the freedom to get stoned, talk bollocks, and believe in hokey bullshit? Plenty of people, apparently. Christiania is a major tourist draw, especially for young drug-loving, festival-going, backpacking types, who make pilgrimages here from all over Europe to worship weed and rightly revel in the thrill of a social alternative co-existing beside the mainstream. Much as I dislike the particular alternative lifestyle on offer in Christiania, I applaud its right to exist – and the implied right for other, better, social alternatives to exist too.

Christiania is outside the law. It also seems to be outside the state. It deems itself an autonomous 'free city', an enclave with rigorously defined borders – neither part of Denmark nor even of the EU. As far as I can make out, it is self-governing. A long-term social experiment, Christiania was set up in the 1970s by free-thinkers who wanted somewhere to practice benign anarchy and smoke lots of drugs. Across 85 acres flanking the upmarket Christianshavn district, they're still getting away with it, despite occasional dark mutterings from the powers that be. Truth is that Christiania's continuing existence has become emblematic of Danish tolerance. The open-minded burghers of Copenhagen would be crazy to close down Christiania now, and thus lose the kudos of allowing it to exist. And anyway, what city in its right mind would want to be so knee-jerk reactionary and paranoid as to close down an enclave which does no harm to the rest of the city, runs pretty smoothly, and even manages to pay for its own street lighting and rubbish collection? Anarchist Christiania actually runs itself much better than a conventionally governed city such as Naples.

I slip in through a side entrance. A psychedelic-fantasy mural filling the side wall of a house tips me off that I'm about to enter the place. Nude fairies flit round a florid tree topped with a mystical flaming egg in a nest, a wise dragon communes with a benign troll clutching a sacred staff, Himalayan peaks rise in the background, and cone-topped circular dwellings dot the middle distance. All the usual brightly-coloured fantasy bullshit. Ugly graffiti tags flank the mural, like rubbish strewn along the edge of a pretty meadow.

I duck down a secretive alley-portal and step out into Christiania itself. Fittingly, a thick stink of cannabis smoke hits me the moment I enter. They must keep a machine pumping a permanent plume of it at arriving visitors, just to establish the right tone immediately. I find myself in a filthy street splattered in low-grade graffiti, reeking of old urine and awash with litter. There are hundreds of bicycles parked outside what claims to be an art gallery (Christiania is completely car-free, one thing it definitely gets right). Many are 'Christiania bikes' – surely the best practical invention to come out of this place. A stout tricycle with a big boxy container between its two front wheels, a Christiania bike is like a cross between a bike and a wheelbarrow. You can fit shopping, kids, or a full-grown friend into the box. The bikes are popular all across Copenhagen and beyond. I've often seen them in Oxford.

I feel a bit like Alice down the rabbit hole, wandering curious and cautious past unfolding oddities. My leafy path snakes past a giant snail shell covered in a mosaic of mirror fragments. Oh I get it. It's an invitation to slow down, to reflect on myself and my unexplored possibilities. Hmmm. Then the 'village' starts to unfurl. Little boutiques hawking trash. Jumbled dwellings. Folk art everywhere. Ragbag decoration from every hippie-loved culture of the world – Jamaican crap, African stuff, Indian things aplenty. Some of it is striking and artful and clever. Much of it is just a mess. Graffiti blooms across every wall and fixed object like a creeping vine, like an organic entity with a life and mind of its own.

I'm terribly disappointed to see lots of signs saying "No photo please". Aw, why no photo?!? I love to take photo! Is the no-photography policy to protect the identity of drug-takers? To safeguard the full-time inhabitants against feeling like zoo-exhibits? (Fair enough.) Maybe even to ensure that visitors keep coming? Christiania preserves a mystique by allowing out no pics. If it was widely seen what a mess this place was, would people still come? Probably. The love of drugs is stronger than the love of tidiness.

Deeper in, I emerge at what must be the village centre – all food-stalls and beer-sellers, shabby marquees and wooden picnic tables. A permanent music-festival vibe. (My worst nightmare!) But there are surprisingly few smiling faces. People seem intent only on getting stoned. Every individual is drinking and smoking – not leisurely, not cheerfully, but determinedly, dogmatically. It is a community of the isolated. Closed, drug-focused, unwelcoming. Not at all what I was expecting. Where are the happy hippies, the laid-back crusties – tedious as hell but undeniably amiable? Confused, and even feeling a little unsafe here, I scramble up a near-vertical dirt path into dense woodland. Trees, darkness, silence.

The path slowly opens out to reveal a sizeable lake – dull grey beneath the leaden sky. Threading my way along the waterside, I discover a widely-spaced series of ramshackle, improvised homes nestling quietly among the leaves. They are an engaging mixture of arty and shambolic – improvised cabins surrounded by teeming plantpots and canoes and jerry-built steps and old tyres and ragged awnings. There are cool, creative things too, like a children's climbing frame nailed together from bits and bobs and cleverly painted with wacky images.

My mind turns vaguely to Thoreau and his book Walden. I say 'vaguely' because I'm not sure if I've ever read it. Something to do with the nobility of simple rustic living, of living alongside nature, in the woods, by a lake – autonomous, free and self-reliant. Permanent camping, basically. I'm struck with a strong sense that there's something admirable about these homes, about this whole part of Christiania. Something healthy and primal. It dawns on me that there are Christianians and Christianians. There are those out here by the water, who hold eco-ideals and other laudable philosophies, who reject the mainstream and believe in a better society, who build homes for themselves and take responsibility and raise open-minded kids and respect their community. Then there are those who spend their days in the centre stoned out of their skulls. Probably there are many in the middle, too, who juggle their desire for both. I spend a long time exploring the woodsy lakeside paths and peering at the secretive cabins, guiltily taking a very small number of photos.

Climbing back down towards the centre, I discover more 'suburban' bits of the colony. Sturdier homes in stone and wood, many of which must have been here long before the 1970s hippie takeover. They're all colourful – decorated with paint and the bright detritus of living. Some are beautiful, with walls in a rich patina of yellow and orange ochre offset by cobalt blue doors. Others sport crazy murals and other improvisations with varying degrees of success. Exotic objects are installed in walls and gardens. Some homes are well-kept. Some are eyesores. But there's an energy and originality to almost all which is impossible not to admire.

What ultimately fascinates me most about Christiania is that this anarchists' colony should be so full of rules. Signs in the woods exhort you not to litter. The centre's ubiquitous "No photo please" signs vie for attention with signs begging you not to urinate (oft ignored, judging by the frequent stink of man-piss). Most interestingly, while the teeming graffiti frequently celebrates cannabis, it equally frequently insists "No hard drugs!" in giant red letters, underscored by pictures of hypodermic needles crossed through with censorious red diagonals. The citizens of Christiania have discovered that no society can exist without rules, without self-control and self-restraint practised by individuals. Ironically, successful anarchy requires laws. Total freedom equals total chaos. There's no freedom without responsibility. The reason Christiania does not unravel is because it self-regulates – like every other successful society. How typical of the orderly Scandinavians that even its anarchists end up running a sustainable community!

Interestingly, as is the case for super-liberal and open societies in general, it is outsiders who almost certainly pose the greatest threat to Christiania, not the free-minded citizens themselves. It is outsiders' temporary exploitation of the unusual freedoms on offer here – without the respect and restraint engendered by living here – that most imperils the reputation and future of the colony. Passing-through, on a bender, thinking only for the short-term, with no sense of responsibility for the place, outsiders bestow on Christiania its greatest uglinesses. Going through the village-centre area on my way toward the exit, I see joyless-faced people passing giant spliffs in a dark marquee and spy the feet of a collapsed stoner crashed out on the floor between its tables. As I step through the main exit onto Copenhagen pavement outside (passing beneath a large sign reading "You are now entering the EU"), I see small groups of boorish men in their 30s, 40s and 50s tumbling paunchily out of taxis with open bottles of beer in their fists, sauntering into Christiania for a night of cerebral impairment. Classy.

The only real criticism I have for Christiania, the only disturbing thing, is that I never felt totally safe in its central parts – particularly as a lone female. And there are very few places in Europe that would ever make me, a hugely experienced solitary traveller, feel that way in full daylight! This is surely the saddest indictment of the place. The fact is, the centre of Christiania is overwhelmingly male-dominated. And these are men who are either shit-faced or intent on getting shit-faced. And travelling in packs. It makes for a menacing atmosphere, no denying it. It breaks my heart that there should be this particular inequality to the place – especially as it sits in Scandinavia, where gender-equality reaches its global zenith! Sigh. Still, for all its vaguely menacing air and its stoners and litter and messy graffiti and hokey art and questionable philosophies, Christiania certainly was bloody interesting, and visiting the place formed the unexpected highlight of this day's exploration of cold, wet Copenhagen.

umbrella girl
paulette mae

"'I cried when you left. What?!! Did I just say that? You slice me open. *I'm glad you came,* you say. My heart flips. I'm in.'"

Paulette Mae is a writer and a dancer, and dances when she writes, you might say...

The sails will slap against the pressure of air, air that is bending, cooling – then teasingly warm. The sails will flap, and I will look from them to you, *they're like...wings. Moth wings.*

And I will remember the night I left the bathroom window open. Left the light on. The heat. I will not see the great white moth clutching the under-sink, invisible until the corner of my eye glimpses the complication of shading and lines against the clinical white. It was the size of a palm. I screamed as if this creature lived within my skin, and then the whole bathroom seemed like the Butterfly House, the one inside Roundhay Park, but full of moths – free, but not free. You will say, ask *wings...wings?* And my moth wings will shoot out into the breeziness above the lake. Louder. Harsher. To reach you. I bend arms up at the elbows, pressing them into my sides. I will transform myself into that great white moth, just for you. *Oh,* you see now. I will fold my wings across my lap. Watch you on the sails around us. You will slide fingers and thumb against each other. Yes, the ones that turn to dust I will tell you. You will mutter something in French. Eyes back on me, then the horizon, wading through fears that I am clingy, will never leave you, you will never be free again.

Their wings were scattered across a lake.

I unfold my knowledge to you. They can't fly now...poor Bombyx Mori. You're smiling when I turn from re-examining the sails. You're dreaming and gathering. Things are falling out of place and cloth that was once tough and hard-wearing, transforms itself into a papery thinness. Even thinner. You feel. You roll in softly, *pa – pil – lon.*

I hear them escaping on your breath.

Papillon. Free. *Watch when they are still,* you say. Pale yellow wings shut against each other. *Like sails.* I re-capture some of the moths I've seen in a memory, and yes – moth wings don't rest in the same way. Do you have to be so literal? I'm thinking. So...exact.

I fear it too. Clinginess. The landing of me upon another. The fluttering, a constant hover. Trying desperately to go the other way. Trying not to succumb to that thought in my head that says anything is possible. Or even possess-able. The only freedom I have is behind glass. But I don't feel anything there. You will allow me in.

My stomach will flip. A change of pressure in the atmosphere. This bowl you call Lake Geneva, or the pond in your garden. Almost. I throw up over the side of the boat. I try my best to make sure what's inside lands in the water only. Ina is very dear to you. I want to throw up all over again. Over the real Ina you named the boat after. I'm hungry. *I'm in the way. I'm in the way* goes off like a siren. Trespassing. It's then I see I'm in your world. On my next retch up, you turn away from the horizon. I'm embarrassed. A fear for Ina, and a fear of me ignites your eyes. But your body is attentive. I take the bottle of water and t-shirt you pull from your bag. Find the courage to say thank you. I'm fine. Really. Honest. I ask for my own bag. You ask if I want to carry on to the shore.

Another side. How many more are there? Getting to you should have been the only one, but then there was getting here, and the rain had started to fall and harden. Outside my window – how do I get there? When the sun is covered by darkening clouds. Locking the door and posting the key, the coach to Heathrow Airport, flight BA0726 bound for you – Project You – then you, then you and a lake. Now it's the other side of its waters. There's a mountain we will climb when we reach. By road? A bus maybe? We will find a cabin. And rest there for the night.

I smile into my compact mirror at the thought of us climbing, and that my face is vomit-free.

I try to relax. Look as if I too, am at one with nature. Calm the storm blackening in my heart. I want to subdue the danger. My parents' assumption that the delicate aren't made for any feat like sailing – anything that can be fallen out of, or off. A bedroom is the safest place in the world. I'm left alone telling Moose off for picking his nose and spreading bogeys on the other teddies in class, or dreaming that my collection of toilet roll middles and bus tickets will soon fill the whole room like water, or learning how to fly. Now I'm sailing. And danger burns on the inside, on the outside. Grey. A shushy TV screen. But the shush fills the room. My bedsit. My insides are red-tinged yellow glowing brighter and brighter. I am an alien here. And besides I have to wear this coat. This grey shushy TV screen coat. It keeps me safe. Keeps them safe out there from any harm. But sometimes I don't want to wear it. I fly as fast as I can to escape its laws. When it rains I stay in. When it's sunny I'm doing everything right. Signs.

I want to feel outside when it's raining.

I glow brighter and brighter when I feel like this. Lava-bright. Beneath all the shush. Sometimes. Few times. Once before. I made it out. Like now. Rising high above reality. Into a fading trail. No wonder you keep giving me that *has-she-just-fallen-out-of-the-sky?* gaze. You offer up something to eat, as if I'm human again. Then you're back with that look of awe and something in your hand. I have to part your fingers to find out what it is. Two squares of chocolate. Your hands must be cold, I say. Mine too. I've never known a man's hands to be cold. You become fragile. Chocolate melts, sticks to the roof of my mouth. Breaks down slowly. I see your movements breaking down too, like a mechanical doll, one part loose, giving way, slowing down, each movement intensifying. And all you're doing is sitting there, arms crossed over the body, playing with your elbow, melting chocolate. But I can see...you're lost, or winding yourself back in. I cried when you left. What?!! Did I just say that? You slice me open. *I'm glad you came*, you say. My heart flips. I'm in.

The water rocks the sun. I dip in fingertips and begin to mould the water, imagine the ripples are the muscles of your back. Your jaguar back now faced my way. Enigmatic. I think that's why I'm here. You want to know, without exploring, what creature this is inside your boat. What creature it is that has followed you here, found you? The water's rolling at us again. There are faster boats on the lake. We have a motor, but you are rowing. I have my head poised over the waters ready. You sense this. Along your spine perhaps? It shifts and then your arm is stretching. And I don't know how, but a hand lands on my shoulder, manages to rub where shoulder meets back. Everything about you is long. Except your fingers. Stubby. Dependable. Strong. *You want to drown yourself.*

What?! I lift my head.

I'll lap water into the hand skimming the water's surface. That water will land in islands on your green t-shirt, warm havens close to your skin. You will look lovely in green. And your scent will be like blood to a vampire. Water is trickling down my back. I slap your leg. Pull you in closer. Like blood to a vampire. These are my vulnerable moments. You hold my hand. My hand. In yours. Or yours in mine. It's hard to tell which bones belong to who, and the cold too, and the heat surfacing. They don't fit in the usual way.

I said something about the sky. Or night? Watching stars through my bedroom window? Crooking back my head with a cheek up against the glass. Sometimes she'd let me out – mum. When dad was away. Playing music for night people. Like me, I guess, without the music. And people – but at least I can do what I want. I've seen them. The pool of darkness they make. Packed together like how I'd imagine my bus tickets and toilet roll middles to pack my room. Moved by me, when I move through them. My dad makes them night people move. But he's quiet. He's not loud like mum. But he makes people move. I'm a bit like dad I think? When I go flying I make things happen. Like that time I made Jason fall off his skateboard. Everyone said he was silly to ride down that hill, *what was he thinking?!* It's really steep and so long people can reach high up above everywhere else (wingless). And there's loads of snickets, and spaces at the side of houses, or between garages, or walls and tall nettles that lead you up higher and higher on the hill that's like a mountain sometimes – Mum says that's why she has big thighs. I don't believe this completely though, because Auntie Annabel has big thighs and it's flat as flat down by her - you can see from up here, and where grandma lives and Kilner Bank and Castle Hill...so Jason seemed really stupid. He can't fly.

But he's really good at lying.

The blood was too red to be real. I hoped it wasn't real – that he'd painted a circle on the side of his face. And it wasn't dry yet. I laughed as brilliant red ran down his face, but he was really crying. I ran away into my room and closed the door. And then quickly opened it again before Dad saw! I went back to Jason then, and called mum, and then...stood staring...catching all his tears in my belly. They washed away whatever it was he did that made me mad.

I wonder if he's going to tell.

I push my head back even more. Searching. My feet go heavy like they're packed with sand, like the ground learned to travel upwards. Into my feet. I choose a star.

You're wondering what to do with me. Now is okay, but what will she expect of me beyond this? I'll expect and desire everything. The wanting and being wanted, the realising some part of you cradles my being, homes it well. In the shy pause, I watch your free hand roaming over the knobbles of our hands joined together. They become something new, a work-in-progress. Kneaded and shaped by a child...or a young heart. Like putty against brown clay. I will ask you what you do for a living. *Errrrr...* funnels down to some point in the distance. Then your mouth fills up again. Faces me trying to claw my way in. I empathise. Your brown eyes return to the distance. You fix boats and sail. You go fishing. You want to say more – or to have more to say. My bones wilt, as they do when I'm asked the same question. Your words are firm, walled high as if to protect the future. Just wanted to sum you up, I suppose. Feel more of your weight. Make you real, credible. I ask you more about the fishing. My granddad used to row *Silver Girl* into the Caribbean Sea. And off Alligator Port he'd drop his fish pot into the waters, look back to the land for three points to find his way back again. To the same spot.

Your eyes soul up.

That's where he caught me, I continue. You seem to know this already. You offer up another two squares of chocolate. So mathematical. Precise. I wonder where your knowing resides, and where your feelings go. Want to tip you out, so we can paddle in your dreams, your sorrow, longings, drive, your...? Maybe I'm jumping here. Flying too far ahead.

(Extract from a novel-in-progress).

brecht's bmw escondido, california

mark axelrod

'Brecht arrived in Hollywood in 1941, with the help of his good friend, Lion Feuchtwanger. But while Feuchtwanger was raking in a lot of Hollywood dough, Brecht was raking banana leaves.'

Axelrod is a California-based author making regular sojourns in Europe with a rucksack full of clean underwear and a head full of literary obsessions. In his witty and doggedly inventive *Borges' Travel, Hemingway's Garage* (2005), from which these pieces are taken, the two things somehow coalesce...

Anyone who knows anything about Brecht's life knows how utterly disappointed Brecht was by failing to make the big bucks as a screenwriter in Hollywood, but what everyone doesn't know is how he finally managed to make a living while he lived there. The truth is truly stranger than fiction.

Brecht arrived in Hollywood in 1941, with the help of his good friend, Lion Feuchtwanger. But while Feuchtwanger was raking in a lot of Hollywood dough, Brecht was raking banana leaves. As a matter of fact, he was so anguished by his failure in Hollywood that he was once quoted as saying *"Jeden Morgen, mein Brot zu verdienen, Gehe ich auf den Markt, wo Lügen gekauft werden. Hoffnungsvoll, Reihe ich mich ein zwischen die Verkäufer."* In English it doesn't sound much better, "Every morning, to earn my bread, I go to the market where lies are bought. Full of hope, I line up among the salesmen." Welcome to Hollywood.

Eventually, Brecht rented a house on 26th Street in Santa Monica about which he wrote, "...[it was] one of the oldest, is about 30 years old, California clapboard, whitewashed, with an upper floor with 4 bedrooms. I have a long workroom (almost 7 meters), which we immediately whitewashed and equipped with 4 tables. There are old trees in the garden (a pepper tree and a fig tree). Rent is $60 per month. $12.50 more than in 25th Street." Meanwhile, in Pacific Palisades, Feuchtwanger was living in the Villa Aurora which even by today's standards is considered opulent. The disparity grated on Brecht who couldn't reconcile how Hollywood valorized the mediocre and relegated intellect to penury.

During his first year in Hollywood, Brecht came up with a number of ideas for screenplays and wrote a number of scripts, including *Joe Fleischhacker*, a collaboration with screenwriter, Ferdinand Reyher. Brecht also worked with Fritz Lang and later with screenwriter, John Wexley. The two of them worked ceaselessly for two months on the final script, but what Brecht discovered 60 years ago works much the same way today. That is, most of what he wrote was discarded and none of his contributions ever got him a film credit. He discovered that Hollywood was not Berlin and wit and intellect were little match in a market that was predicated on glitz. To that end, Eisenstein's words ring true. (See: *Eisenstein's Café*).

Enter Hemingway. By accident, Brecht's car broke down in Santa Ana while on a weekend outing to Laguna Beach. As fate would have it, AAA towed the car to Hemingway's Garage (see *Borges' Travel, Hemingway's Garage*) when Hemingway himself showed up. Coincidentally,

Hemingway was also on his way to Laguna Beach to look for property to purchase for a café. While they worked on his car, Hemingway and Brecht had breakfast at DaVinci's Restaurant and after Brecht relieved himself of all that troubled him about being a screenwriter, Hemingway suggested that he "Fuck Hollywood and the screenwriters" since "they're all Jews anyway." He went on to say, "You can make some decent dough selling BMWs in Southern California and if you play your cards right, get laid in the process."(1)

Brecht didn't think much about the idea since he was practically broke, but Hemingway said he'd help bankroll the business. So the oddest couple of all, (2) Hemingway and Brecht, opened Brecht BMW in the fall of 1942. Brecht managed the business for several years making enough money to return to Switzerland in 1947 the day after his appearance before the House Un-American Activities Committee on 30 October 1947. Before he left the US, he opined that he was saddened by the fact the HUAC didn't interrogate him on Halloween since "what better day to carry out a witch hunt." (3)

Though he sold his share of the franchise shortly before he left the country, the dealership remains in his name today and can be found in Escondido, California.

(1) *From Carburetors to Carbohydrates: Hemingway's Orange County Businesses*. I.M. Slavish. Newport Beach, CA: OC Publishing, 2001. Hemingway was alluding to the wealthy, widowed Orange County women who preferred BMW to Mercedes; however, what Hemingway didn't know then, but was to learn later, was that Brecht "liked to hit from both sides of the plate."

(2) The Hemingway-Brecht relationship was the initial idea behind the Matthau-Lemmon film, *The Odd Couple*, directed by Gene Saks, written by Neil Simon.

(3) *Bluster & Bull Shit: Brecht's Hollywood Diaries*. Kurt Weill. Boston: Harvart Press, 1949.

da vinci's ristorante tustin, california

mark axelrod

'As a matter of fact, it is now known that the Mona Lisa was actually modeled on a woman who was to become his first waitress!'

Ah, Da Vinci...inventor, military engineer, sculptor, illustrator, architect, scientist, restaurateur. Restaurateur? Yes, it was the Da Vinci no one knew about, but it was only a matter of time before Da Vinci would open a restaurant since food was so important to him. As a matter of fact, it is now known that the Mona Lisa was actually modeled on a woman who was to become his first waitress!(1)   It's also patently clear by the subject matter of his paintings: *The Last Supper*, 1497; the *Proportions of the Human Figure*, 1490 (which was originally titled the *Proportions of the Human Waiter*); the restaurant in the background of St. Jerome, 1480; the restaurant in the foreground of the *Annunciation*, originally commissioned for Verrocchio, 1478; the background of the uncompleted, *Adoration of the Magi*, 1482; and the recently discovered sketch books, titled *Coglioneria: Sketches of a Frustrated Restaurateur*. In the sketch book, Da Vinci had designed over 236 different restaurants in hopes that some day he might have his own.

This all came to a head 8 April 1476 when Leonardo, then 24, and several others were denounced to the police for having "committed sodomy" with a 17-year old model named Jacopo Saltarelli. The anonymous accusation was found in tamburo outside the Palazzo Vecchio and read that Saltarelli "...consents to please those persons who request such wickedness of him" and that he had "served several dozen people." The assumption was that Saltarelli was a male prostitute and though the case came before the courts twice, it was dismissed on both occasions. But the truth was Leonardo and Saltarelli eventually became lovers!

In a recently published book titled *Lui gli ha fatto una bella pipa* (2) it is clear that they had remained lovers for decades and eventually moved to California where, Leonardo thought, homosexuality would be more tolerated. In 1516, a 40-year old Leonardo and a 33-year old Saltarelli, with some funding from Lorenzo di Pietro de' Medici, both sailed to California on board one of Colon's ships, the *La Quaglia* which was headed for the port of San Francisco. Unfortunately, their cartographer became confused and they ended at what is now known as Laguna Beach. What they discovered was a haven for homosexuals and they bought a bungalow there before making their way inland to Tustin where Leonardo fulfilled his desire of opening his own restaurant (and, eventually, a motel) due to the astute real estate savvy of Saltarelli who opened his own real estate agency there as well. But in June, 1518, Leonardo was recalled to Italy to plan the festival at Amboise for the wedding of Lorenzo di Pietro de' Medici and Madeleine de La Tour d'Auvergne. Though he had full intentions of returning to Tustin, that never happened. In January, 1519, he became sick and only a few months later, he died. Hearing of Leonardo's death some months later, Saltarelli could not face living in Italy without Leonardo and remained in Tustin where he continued to own and operate all three businesses. As living testimony to both of them, the businesses remain to this day.

(1) *From Lasagne Magro to Mona Lisa: The Waitress Behind the Genius* Carlo Emilio Calvino. Milan: Edizioni Scola, 2002.

(2) *Lui gli ha fatto una bella pipa.* Luchresi Rizzarsi. Edizione Foccaccia. Translated by Mark Axelrod as *The Saltarelli Diaries.* Tustin, CA: Saltarelli Press, 2003.

the babel anthology

fieldwork

Our section for work somewhere between essay and literature or even, as in the case of *Peckham Tales*, anthropology/social history.

peckham meat tales: john dell of head's butchers & rye lane/ bushmeat

gareth stanton

'Police suspect that places selling bushmeat might also be sources of human meat to be used in witchcraft.'

Stanton is a British anthropologist of the post-colonial generation who has sought to apply the insights of this revolutionary junior science to a world other than that playground of younger sons and Oxbridge eccentrics, the British Empire. Eventually the grown-ups will catch up with him. Meanwhile here is one of his bulletins from 'The Jungle of the Cities' as another provincial bright spark, Bertolt Brecht, called it... (Extracted from a longer academic piece.)

John is well known to his customers. For many he is the last remaining vestige of something which makes them think of their past, the glorious past of Rye Lane when it was a shopping hub for south-east London and shoppers came from miles around. Now that is all gone, some say, with the exception of John. No doubt this is a rose-tinted version of the past, but it is easy to see how this happens. John, simply, fails to abide by the normally accepted rules of the contemporary commercial game.

He knows many of his customers by name and is prepared to spend considerable amounts of time in conversation. For a certain segment of his clientele he is the focus of the community. People waiting in the often lengthy queue will greet each other and exchange pleasantries in a way that they ordinarily would not do on the street. Whether you desire an expensive leg of lamb or simply a rasher of bacon it is all the same to John, he is equally interested in you. John could have expanded his trade hugely over recent decades, but he chooses not to. He likes his enterprise to be small scale, caring even, in the sense that that word once had, back in the mists of time. He makes his own sausages and chipolatas, grinds the cuts of beef for his own burgers, the antithesis of Schlosser's *Fast Food Nation* (2001). Recent events, however, have threatened to destabilize his choices. To understand this, it is necessary to be aware that John is a figure from a different era in more ways than one. If the huge *halal* butchers which dominate Rye Lane in its most recent incarnation bring a new style of meat preparation to the world of south-east London, then another trend of long standing has been the increasing decline of the family butcher, first in the face of the chain butchers, but now in the shape of the butcher's counters at the big supermarkets, where the rationalization and profit maximization motives have resulted in forms of de-skilling that reach their apogee in Schlosser's world of the Big Mac.

The truth of the matter is that John Dell is a qualified master butcher, a craftsman of his trade. There is no other shop selling meat on Rye Land that doesn't have it all displayed in its full bloody finery, wrapped in cling film, or simply in un-refrigerated stacks, exuding an odour that many passing on the street find repellent. With John you have to ask what's good or if he has the cut you want. If he does, he goes out to the cold store and brings the meat to the counter to cut off the required quantity. The meat is then trimmed and the rest returned to cold storage, out of sight of customers. Some of them, then, were surprised by an article in the *Evening Standard* on 28 December 2002, entitled 'Meaty role for butcher', accompanied by John's photo. As they must have been by the appearance, around the same time, of a

Sky broadcast van outside the shop. Until this point, Peckham's most famous butcher had been south-east London boy Michael Caine, in the film adaptation of Graham Swift's *Last Orders*. While that fictional shop was set in Bermondsey, the filming, as stated previously, took place in Bellenden Road in Peckham. Scorsese's *Gangs of New York* spent several years under raps before getting a general release. For this period of time, John had been guarding a secret. His clientele range from frail old-age pensioners living in council accommodation to those living in the magnificent Georgian houses which line the Rye itself.

A film producer living in one of these houses had recognized John's exceptional qualities behind his modest demeanour and had recommended John to be the man to train Daniel Day Lewis in the necessary butchering skills needed for his role in the film. Duly, during the course of filming, he had been flown out to Rome on successive weekends, put up in a five-star hotel and chauffeured to the set for the training sessions. John had not felt able to spend longer periods in Italy because he felt that this would have meant letting down his customers back in Peckham. John enjoyed his time working on the film and, on parting, gave Day Lewis the old and worn filleting knife that he had first acquired in the days when he too was learning his trade.

Wandering down Rye Lane there are numerous outlets for halal meat, along with a number of the commercial chains. In the face of this competition John is serene. In truth, they do not represent competition and John only bemoans the lack of butchering skill in the modern world. His customer base is secure. Many of John's regulars are members of the Peckham Society, and he represents a contemporary manifestation of the nostalgic projection into the past represented by the Society in its battle for the integrity of Peckham, past and present.

He is the hub of a complex network of Peckhamites who find questions of history interesting and who invest issues of local history with cultural capital. One day he will be gone, and writers to the Peckham Society will talk of the days of real butchers on Rye Lane. This work of nostalgic memory can be seen in this context as a defence against change. It acts like a chemical fixative, generating a single image out of a molecular chaos. Is that fleeting image what we call community?

Rye Lane/bushmeat

The shops in Rye Lane are in a constant state of flux. The many nations involved in their workings are invoked in the names, in the profusion of goods, the 'exotic' products. Many strangers who venture here for the first time are astounded by the variety of edible goods on sale, not that they would be eating them. Most commented upon is the dried fish and the land snails dried and skewered on sticks. The latter are sometimes for sale alive (special farms have grown up in the UK). Those of a suspicious frame of mind suggest the sale of bushmeat. It is the possible presence of such a commodity which marks out the slow transition of many of the shops on Rye Lane from one of predominantly Caribbean influence to something with a less mediated African quality. Africa is, of course, a mere spectre, and individual shops stock more regional choices, something to be seen from the displays of videos available, which give some pointer to any national or ethnic affiliations. The reality is rather more difficult to pin down, the number of nationalities is stupefying. The increasing retail presence of many African-run shops, however, raises the ire of less recent arrivals, who comment on the smell (which, in fact, comes mostly from dried stock fish).

Meat and practices surrounding meat are great symbolic markers and strictly policed in the West. While it is permissable for Shrek and Princess Penelope to eat cane rat in the movies, for many in the West bushmeat is the antithesis of food, and this is why streets such as Rye Lane (and other London markets such as Brixton or Ridley Road) sometimes disturb. While the trade in such products may bring in disease, and while it does have serious ecological consequences in Africa and would appear to be increasingly commercialized in order to feed growing markets for such products in the West, it still has the power to invoke an Africa of the European imagination. The consumption of monkeys and even primates more closely related to humans, such as chimpanzees, brings in another spectre. In October 2002, the magazine *Environmental Health News* carried a piece entitled 'Human flesh tip-off triggers raid'. In a raid on a shop in Tottenham in north London two tons of unfit meat had been seized (including a crocodile head). Police suspect that places selling bushmeat might also be sources of human meat to be used in witchcraft. As the author notes, 'Rumours have been circulating for some time that human flesh may be in some north London boroughs for ritual purposes'. Those arrested for bushmeat offences in Ridley Road market the year before resided in East Dulwich, close to Rye Lane.

the babel anthology

the babel anthology
poems & shorts

notes

Heathcote Williams is a great Englishman in ways the *Daily Mail* could never dream of. Consistently he has done something more than 'speak truth to power', he has spoken truth to all of us in our little powers, which add up potentially to form a great power. The choice he poses here between destroying ourselves and the shared environment or embracing a technology far more wonderful and liberating than self-parking Beamers or any other roadstinkers is in the same stream as his great work *Autogeddon*. Thanks to Huxley Scientific Press, Oxford, for this poem taken from H.W.'s *Forbidden Fruit* (2011).

Tes Noah Asfaw has recently completed a screenplay, now working on his first novel. Tes is short for Tesfaye, an Ethiopian name. We can only hope that, one day, Tes finds Gee-zus after writing this despicably irreverent piece. We will pray for him.

Ray Keenoy with yet another tribute to Orwell (see his *The Moon Under Water*).

D.B. Fishman's poem on a legendary jazzer echoes a rich literary theme: the maimed give birth to beauty, joy even...

Adam Flint is from Oxford but not an Oxford type (you know what we mean). This is a tribute to another Frenchman – Antonin Artaud – who bedazzled and inspired and even terrified... And then he (Adam) found himself in the short-stay car park, terror upon terror.

Wild name, wild writing! Youthful and slightly testy **Calypso Blaj** bares her teeth in a sexy way here.

Dr. Kathleen M. Quinlan is a member of the *Back Room Poets* in Oxford, along with **Deborah Mason** and **David Olsen**. The BRPs maintain a facebook page for their readings and events.

Translator and author **C. J. Young** says of this piece: 'Each composition is influenced by the timbre of words and the distinct flavour of a moment. I believe that the modern lyric poem can be the space of an authentic connection between readers without having to be explicit or confessional'.

heathcote williams

all bikes are weapons

All bikes are weapons,
Making cyclists warriors
Who kick pollution
With their miracle
Machines that recycle greed –
Revolutionary
Wheels spinning around
Trillions and trillions of times
All on empty tanks –
Just an airy lungful
Pumped tightly into two tubes
Causing nothing but
Exhilaration
And liberation, instead of
Trails of filth and death.
On their bikes wise clowns
Keep pneumatic hoops gyrating
In perfect balance.
Oil rigs aren't blown up.
There's no spillage in the seas
From bicycle wars.
Bicycle power
Produces no exhaust fumes.
No carcinogens.
Man-powered machines

Are anti-capitalist –
You can't meter air.
The bicycle is the
The most efficient machine
Ever created:
Stored up calories
Become gas – three thousand
Miles per gallon.
Bikes are subversive:
"Governments must help get rid
Of cars so that bikes
Can eliminate
Government" Dutch anarchists
Wrote in Amsterdam.
Few are unhappy
On bikes. People get angry
In their deadly cars.
On a recumbent
Bike the top speed is
A hundred and thirty-
Two kilometers
Per hour which, by rights, should make
Oil quite redundant.
While big oil clings to
Motorised suicide-bombs
For man's transport
Revolving bike wheels
Postpone the end of the world –

Second by second.
'Nothing compares to
The simple pleasure of a
Bike ride.' J. F. K.
If he'd stuck to bikes
And ignored Dallas limos
He'd have lived longer.
What a decision!
Bicycles run on fat and
They save you money –
Cars run on money
And they make you fat.
A difficult choice.

tes noah asfaw
goodboy

I shot god today. You know, the cute-looking creatures that only children (and adults left sprawled flat in desperate rescue of their marbles) would seem to adore. There are millions of god, the one family with a plurality of genera but a unified consciousness; a solitary soul. To shoot god is nigh on impossible but when you do it reverberates amongst all its bodies instantaneously. And god never dies; god recovers. God remembers.

I carry the limp body to the temple of our frail deity and lay it at the altar. This will be our first offering to Him in seven months. Our song echoes in the hallowed expanse and in the crevices of our ancient Pagoda. The hymn guides us: Dog will strengthen in all His glory and deliver us from the treacheries of this world. He will maintain our haven from the growing hostility of god. I turn to face the congregation and lift up my arms as tears jog down my cheeks and filter through my collar. How beautiful it is to know conviction as pure as this. Then I notice her. The girl. No more than six. Giggling. Her eyes following a line of action yet to be discovered by any of us in spiritual rapture. I turn. God had gone. The limp body had arisen and escaped. The child had borne witness to it, had delighted in seeing cute in motion. I exclaim loudly. My congregation follows suit with wails of appeals and challenges. What shall we do? To whom shall we turn for salvation?

The measured cadence of our mourning is pierced by squeals of ebullience from the doorway. All of our children are stood there. They are looking out into the field, at god. In return, god, in its vast numbers, sit silently, waiting, watching. Angry. We believe that god does not differentiate between adult and child, between instigator and innocent. We believe that god will kill us all one day, as presaged by the swell of their numbers these recent years and the bold reduction of their distance from us with each and every failed sacrifice. Nevertheless, the children are jubilant. They stroke each other's heads in mock trials of the dreams they daren't mention to their elders. The dreams of cherishing god as pet, god as a beloved. The most fervent of my believers turns to her neighbour. We were all that way once. Yes.

In time the healthy shoots of Cynicism will grow within each one of them, as per the Scriptures. And their natural affinity for evil, for god, shall be displaced by an unbridled devotion to our Good Boy.

ray keenoy
in praise of pubs

I mean those places that are slightly gloomy, where the music, if not
just the lull of voices and the clink of glass, stays muted
and, most important;

a space that is somehow long, in the form of the classic Public Bar;

a narrow place, wider than it is deep.

A space where thoughts have room to travel.

After the first pint, you'll stand by the river and,
looking back down it, touch the past,
its comforts and its blunted hurts,

after the second, more stimulated, the mind reaches up to the future

following the smiling swallow on his wonder-voyage
to dangerous and pleasurable *unknowns*.

But on the third,

as the seams of the everyday and sober garment start to rend,

there is the most giddy turn of all: back down to *the present*
and its genuine, unsustainable, excitements.

d.b. fishman
flowers for django

The eighteen year old Manouche
Traversing night after a performance
Returns to his new wife, to his caravan
Filled with the thick waxen curves
Of flowers made of celluloid, for selling,
But bending down at the sound
Of some phantom mouse, the candle
Drops, lighting the touchpaper –
Engulfed in the roar of flame
They somehow collapse into air
But the right leg, the left arm burned
The gypsy's half the man he was
With only two-fingered mobility -
Tendons on the left hand, shrunk
In the heat, pinning
The other two to the palm –
Recuperating, he creates
A new technique, for two-fingered soloing
Following American jazz, improvising
Never the same solo twice;
This calm, dapper Belgian
With immaculate moustache,
Those fingers seizing, gripping
The strings like angered birds,
Spritely letting fly those
Jumping runs of notes
At belief-defying speed –
Swift and graceful –
To mastery of his craft

calypso blaj
something going

And all I wish I could do is tear it up over and over again till the splinters break and there is nothing left but your core sheltered inside the kernel. I wish I could tear you to pieces till I watch your soul break, to feed the hungry dogs salivating at your flesh. You don't know what I can do with a sledgehammer, but I can show you. If you only asked, I would show you how violently I can swing it till I dent you so many times and make you feel what is shaking me. I'll slap you against a wall and bite you, beat you, throw at you, furrow the compass into your flesh and brand a circle so you know what it means. Do you know how to care? There's an arid space floating around between the walls of your chest waiting for paraffin. I want to stick my fist in it and stab the needle so many times you'll never forget what I have and what I do and what I am.

It's all so tense and pulsating and you don't know what to do with yourself. I taught you what to do with oil and butter but your hands are still clumsy. You don't know how to smile. When you look at me there's a gap and I don't know what to do. I want to string a thread from you to me, but I'm sick of you. Why do you pressure me? Or rather, why do you not? I loathe you, I wish your bones were stiffer. I want me to change... but God knows I've tried that. Take an axe and cut your trunks, just start over because you're not enough and I want more.

I want to drink you. Feel your lips and the wetness on your fingers, but you know I can't be taken. You tried, I pitied. This is what it is. Again and again and again and again and again, I pity and I let you spin. But do you think this is enough? I'm not happy and I'll make the connections broader than you think. I can do so much but you don't know how to move. Throw the pebble on the water but there's a voraciously throbbing ocean sucking hard and mutating with every ejection. I want more and the pebbles aren't enough. My revenge is constant, gratify it I said, but your fingers are too small.

bit.ly/LEAOa9 finds more of C.B.'s work.

deborah mason
nunnery night

Stepping out of the nunnery
full of warmth and red wine
into the dark white shroud
of a freezing midnight fog,
I'm suddenly like a nun
after Vatican Two:
no longer enclosed.
Outside these protective walls
I'm half-shrouded, half-exposed.

The world has changed
while I've been inside:
boundaries are no longer clear.
This brave new world's full
of uncertainties; slippery
as a fish; ungraspable.
The lamplight's dim;
its glow's diffused by fog.

Black habit or plain clothes,
it's all the same tonight.
All roads may lead to Rome
but will they lead me home
this cold-white, nun-dark night?

david olsen
raven

My former best friend
and latter-day worst enemy waits.
To him I've surrendered more

than most people ever possess.
My travelling companion
to wherever I call home

is nominally 12 years old
but, unopened, has matured
to 13 ... 14 ... 14½.

An ever-accusing presence
on dresser, desk or shelf,
the raven is vigilant, challenging.

A glass, poor Yorick?
Mr Laphroaig's little joke.
Go to hell. I can be brave

in the afternoon's test of will
when I forget that I still
have to make it through the night.

NB: 'Laphroaig'™ is a single malt whisky.

adam flint

antonin

Artaud –
a glove puppet
in dire need of darning popped
his head above the tabletop
in the lounge bar
on the scrounge for
surrender
nobody
had to give.

absence report (extract)

Start Date: 01/02/05
End Date: 02/02/05
Days: 2
Absence Description: Viral illness
Absence Notes: Viral infections

Warm, white russian palms
cupping thought like an alms bowl.
Eyes: two headless coins
melting in the hollow
Buckingham arm of the canal
beyond the short-stay car park …

dr. kathleen m. quinlan
the question

It used to take a different form when I was a young woman

narrow at waist and wide at hip; fertile.

"Do you want to – ?"

I could see the pages turning – knew how the story would go for the hero

and his Eve or Mary, following unexamined plot lines of religion or biology.

It was easy to answer then, when

the blank pages of my yet un-authored life

lay waiting for me to compose a different legacy.

I'm not sure which clock tick or grey hair rephrased it:

"Did you ever want to – ?"

Now I stumble trying to be true to the way it has hung,

like mother's fur coat in the back of the cupboard;

pulled out, tried on, inspected, and put back again,

behind the everyday wear

for as long as I've had a womb.

Instead, I flip back through the chapters, looking for clues to the bequest that does not have

my soulful brown eyes or stubborn, independent streak.

I read between the lines of thought in search of knowing: probing that white space

on which graphite is laid down stiffly and taken up in rubbery strands;
what could not be erased.

And there, deep in the pressed, bleached tree fibers is a mother
making way for something else to grow inside her and be born.

surrendering to a dream

Our first kiss nearly knocked me off the fallen-log seat,
as the creek gurgled a quiet serenade.

We abandoned shoes and good sense to wade in the stream,
holding hands to steady ourselves against algae's treachery.

We bent over in the tiny waterfall and felt the
current's surprising force as it massaged our arms and legs.

We stood at the base of a raging cascade -
wet in its blanket-spray – like diamonds.

We imagined the ocean lying ahead,
downstream, shared.

c.j. young

I.

Darkness thick with laurel:

a rustle of waxy tongues

in wrought iron cages.

Human shadows hasten

along the white avenue, which cools

at leisure, muffling lower taste.

The air stirs, clean and strange;

I am passing through.

Half a block away, the headlights

hiss like a broken wave

eternally groping for land.

deborah mason
flash fiction: car park

They had been looking for a suitable place for a picnic for some time when Jane spotted a handwritten notice pinned to a tree: CARPARK.

A wobbly arrow pointed along a dirt track into the forest. It seemed an odd place for a car park, but, Jane said hopefully, "There might be toilets." She did not like going behind bushes on picnics. They drove along the bumpy track until they came to a clearing. There were no other cars in sight: only a huge, wooden boat. Stephen parked the car. As they walked towards the boat, they saw there was an aquarium built into it, full of gold and white fish swimming through a submerged, miniature world.

A notice was taped to a money box fixed to the boat: DONATIONS GRATEFULLY RECEIVED. Below, in smaller letters, was written: PLEASE DO NOT FEED THE CARP.

the babel anthology

french collection

the babel anthology

three stories from médan

introduced & selected by sylvain atiocha

Sylvain Atiocha got on the scent of *the babel anthology* early and, before disappearing to the ends of the Earth à la his hero Rimbaud (though we have no direct evidence he is presently running guns), he suggested the greater part of the French material in *tba1* as well as writing this introduction to three pieces from a little-known collection of pieces by Zola and his literary fellow-travellers.

on 'les soirées de médan'
sylvain atiocha

What Rimbaud did for poetry, Zola did for prose. The great contemporary American poet John Ashbery recently said if we are absolutely modern, it is because Rimbaud' s work urged us to be, and still does. The same could be said of Zola, and the movement he belonged to – naturalism. Naturalism is best defined in opposition to classicism: it was a revolutionary force in literature because it liberated the writer from established forms and modes of thought (such as nationalism: all the stories in *Les Soirées de Médan* are set during the Franco-Prussian war, but are deliberately non-patriotic).

In this respect, all literature since Zola, even the most fantastic, is indebted to his example. But the most significant achievement of naturalism is a commitment – political and social as well as literary – to the description of ordinary life. This is not exclusively proletarian art of the fascist-soviet variety, but a willingness to describe things as they are: ugly. In a world where our information is selected for us, Zola is one example of a counterforce. Of course, this schema is simplistic – they were others before Zola, like Balzac, and Chekhov is another good example.

But in the history of literature, Zola and his generation of realists mark a turning point; this revolutionary commitment to realism is what makes 19th century literature relevant as well as enjoyable. A note on the title: naturalism did not really exist as a movement, it was more of a tendency diagnosed *a posteriori*. But the writers the term enfolds knew each other, and were aware of the significance of their new aesthetic.

The book's title combines friendship and literature, as Médan was the name of Zola' s house on the outskirts of Paris where they would sometimes gather.

the attack on the mill (from 'l'attaque du moulin')

émile zola

Translated by C.J. Young

'A lock had been built there which spouted water from a height of several metres onto the millwheel, which made a creaking noise as it turned, like the asthmatic cough of a loyal servant who had grown old in the house. When someone suggested to old Merlier that he should change it, he shook his head and said that a young wheel would be lazier and not so well acquainted with the job.'

Regrettably, Zola's name in the Anglo world at least, has been captured by the pop charlatans behind a tasteless musical but this little-known piece (in a new translation by C.J. Young) demonstrates his powerful prose style, both fluent and lyrical.

the babel anthology

That fine summer's evening, old Merlier's mill was a scene of celebration. Three tables had been placed end-to-end in the courtyard, in anticipation of the guests. The occasion was common knowledge in the village: Merlier's daughter, Françoise, was to be engaged to Dominique, a lad whom some accused of being a layabout, but whose gentlemanly charm won him the adoring gaze of every woman within a three-league radius.

This mill of old Merlier's was a delightful picture, standing right in the middle of Rocreuse, at a bend in the main road. It was the village's only road, in truth; a row of simple dwellings flanked it on either side. But there at the apex of the bend, a view opened onto fields and lofty trees which lined the banks of the Morelle, dappling the bottom of the valley with gorgeous shade. It was the most charming piece of nature in all Lorraine. To the left and to the right, thick woods and ancient forests covered the gentle slopes, filling the horizon with a sea of greenery, while straight ahead, the bounteous plain stretched ever southwards, unrolling its patchwork of fields and hedgerows seemingly to infinity. But what made Rocreuse truly lovely was the coolness which nestled in this verdant hollow even during the hottest days of July and August. As the Morelle flowed down through the woods of Gagny, it seemed to take on the pleasant chill of the canopy which covered it for those leagues. It brought with it the forest's murmuring noises and its cold, reverential shade. And it was by no means the only cooling water to babble among the woods; indeed, there was a new gushing spring to discover at every step. As one walked the wood's narrow paths, one could almost sense a subterranean lake trying to pierce through the moss, searching for the slightest cracks between the rocks and at the feet of trees through which to burst forth in crystalline fountains. The whispering voices of these streams were so many and so loud that they drowned out the song of the bullfinches. One felt as though one were in an enchanted park, with waterfalls cascading all around.

Gigantic chestnut trees cast their dark shadows in the damp meadows below. At the edges of the fields, long rows of poplars formed great rustling curtains. Two avenues of plane trees marched across the countryside towards the ancient, ruined Château de Gagny. In this perpetually watered earth, the grass grew wildly tall. The land between the two wooded slopes thus resembled a garden, but a natural one, in which the meadows were the lawns and the stands of huge trees stood in for beds of flowers. When the midday sun shone directly overhead, the trees took on a bluish tint and the blazing grass bent over in the heat, while an icy thread ran past beneath its canopy.

And that was where the cheerful tick-tock of old Merlier's mill could be heard, in that hollow of wild greenery. The construction, made of beams and plaster, seemed as old as time itself and was half-immersed in the Morelle, which rounded out at that point to form a clear basin. A lock had been built there which spouted water from a height of several metres onto the millwheel, which made a creaking noise as it turned, like the asthmatic cough of a loyal servant who had grown old in the house. When someone suggested to old Merlier that he should change it, he shook his head and said that a young wheel would be lazier and not so well acquainted with the job. He mended the old one with whatever he had to hand: barrel staves, rusty metal bands, scraps of zinc and lead. The wheel seemed happier for it, with its irregular profile, plumed with grass and moss. When it was struck by the silvery jet of water, it appeared to be covered with beads. Its odd frame, as it turned, seemed to pass through a glistening curtain composed of dangling strings of pearls.

The part of the mill which bathed thus in the Morelle resembled a primitive ark, run aground in that very spot. A good half of the dwelling had been built on stilts; the water ran beneath the floor. There were holes in the floor through which, the villagers told, eels and gigantic crayfish could be caught. Beneath the lock, the pool was as clear as a mirror, and when it was not disturbed by the foaming of the wheel, some big fish could be seen slowly patrolling the water in squadrons. A broken staircase descended to the river, where a boat was moored to a stake. A wooden gallery crossed above the millwheel. Windows opened here and there at irregular intervals in the wall. All in all it was a pell-mell of corners, little jutting walls and tacked-on extensions, beams and sections of roofing which gave the mill all the appearance of an ancient, dismantled citadel. But ivy and all kinds of climbing plants had grown over it, filling in the larger cracks and covering the old home with a green cloak.

The young women who passed by would sketch old Merlier's mill in their albums. On the road side, the house was sturdier. A stone doorway opened onto a large courtyard, which was flanked on both sides by granaries and stables. Next to a well stood a great elm which provided shade for half the courtyard. Behind it stood the house proper, with its row of four upstairs windows, topped by a dovecote. Old Merlier's only affectation was to have the front of the house whitewashed every ten years. It had just been painted, and when the sun shone in the middle of the day, the village was dazzled by it.

the babel anthology

the incident at the '7' (from 'l'affaire du grand 7')

léon hennique

Translated by C.J. Young

"*Bagasse!*" exclaimed a soldier from Marseilles.'

Hennique (1851-1935) was a joyful young Bohemian, one of a great creative generation that included Huysmans and Maupassant. An admirer and protege of Zola he deserted him during the great man's travails (*J'Accuse!*) over the Dreyfus affair, after writing a novel about airships with the unlikely title *La Devouée,* articles on spiritualism and telepathy as well as theatrical work. This piece, considered to be one of the best in the entire *Les Soirées* collection, transmits the furious, cynical and almost surreal anti-militarism of the young Hennique. (RK)

"The Prussians are twenty leagues away," he announced. "The sergeant expects that every man will do his duty."

Nobody believed the news. It was welcomed by a cold silence, which before long was noisily interrupted by the sounding of the lights-out in the barracks' courtyard. Since the invasion, this had occurred every night at a half past eight. It was a calm, resonant sort of sound, gentle at first. Two notes were repeated three times, followed by a piercing, melancholy phrase. Previously, the bugle's call had rung out in the long, light evenings of August. Now, as autumn set in, it belonged instead to the gaunt, dim twilight. The alert began once more, then the same sad phrase, wavering as it died away.

The Lieutenant was standing outside the door. "Look," he said, "It's the Northern Lights. Look, Briottet!"

"Oh yes! Marvellous, Lieutenant, quite marvellous!" replied the Sergeant-Major. Beyond the closed door, a murmur faded as they moved away.

Two minutes later, the whole garrison came running to gather in the courtyard, forming an almost peaceful crowd. A few white shirts stood out in the darkness.

"*Bagasse!*"[1] exclaimed a soldier from Marseilles.

His comrades were content just to watch. Enclosed on three sides by the enormous *corps de logis* and its two wings, the courtyard opened to the north like a square cave-mouth. Framed in the sky before them, a glowing sheet was advancing imperceptibly on the town, which stood beyond the barracks' fence and the huge, deserted parade ground, already lit pink. The sheet appeared to billow upwards, stretching out in parallel with a straight road, melting into the pallor of the atmosphere. A thousand wispy vortices began to loop themselves at its edges. At the point where a second road intersected the first, the thin line of the distant horizon glowed with such fiery intensity that it resembled the furious muzzle flash of a great artillery piece. A few chimneys and the ridges of a few roofs were brushed with a bronze tint. Somewhere, in some far-off yard, a dog was barking. In front of the barracks' fence, an armed sentry was pacing slowly, the tip of his bayonet glinting now and then with brief, sharp flashes.

"There's blood in the air," says a soldier. "There must be fighting somewhere."

| A distinctive regional expletive.

"No, it's the good Lord having a nosebleed," came the rejoinder from one of his comrades.

"Ha! It could be a fire," Sauvageot pointed out.

"That looks like a fire to you, does it?"

The group jeered at Sauvageot. Corporal Verdier silenced them angrily.

"Shut up! Bloody fools, you're going to get me sent to the slammer!"

At the other side of a second courtyard, behind the barracks' main façade, the lights-out sounded for a second time. Dulled by the distance, the bugle's call took on a pitiful tone. It sounded somehow dead, a sound cast out of that blazing sky like a piece of jetsam. The windowpanes of the barracks, already filled with vague reflections, were gradually being illuminated by the sky.

Meanwhile, some distance from the group formed by the soldiers and as far as possible from the Corporal, two friends had launched into their own conversation.

"So, then, you bumped into Joliot…"

"On my way back, after I took the soup to the prison."

"Why hasn't he come back?"

"He got hold of some local money."

"Ah! The devil."

"He wanted to take me along to break bread with him at old mother Mathis'."

"And you turned your nose up?"

"No thanks, I'm just out of jail… God, aren't we getting old?"

"Are you a man or a mouse?"

There was a silence before Joliot's admirer continued: "Where's he sleeping? Have you any idea?"

"At the 7, no less!"

"Ah! The devil."

The conversation ended in broken laughter. But just as the lights-out sounded for the third time, yet further away, with a noise like that of a toy trumpet, Corporal Verdier said:

"Right then, boys, let's get some sleep, shall we?"

Everybody went back inside. The candle was flickering its last on the trestle table; Verdier put it out. There was a strange, sleepy heaviness in the air. Nobody wanted to speak. The dark silence was disturbed only by the rustle of uniforms being removed and the knocking of boots as they were dropped carelessly to the floor. All of a sudden, Sauvageot cried out:

"Won't this miserable war be over soon? What's the use of it, really? Things were going so nicely before!"

Just then, as the bedsteads creaked under the weight of the soldiers' tired bodies, a trooper broke wind noisily.

"Forget it, Sauvageot."
Sauvageot was not deterred. He spoke again, more firmly this time:

"I mean, war... What's the use of it?"

He was about to continue his whinging when Verdier ordered:

"Silence!"

Within a quarter of an hour, everyone was asleep. The tall, thin soldier and the Corporal were snoring in alternation.

Little by little, a reddish light crept in through the window. Pale at first, it soon became dazzling as it slipped towards the nearest bed, marking it as if with a bloody stain. Directly above the barracks, the sky was being invaded by the Northern Lights.

rucksack (from 'sac au dos')

joris-karl huysmans

Translated by C.J. Young

Huysmans participated in the Franco-Prussian war and was a young disciple of Zola and his Naturalism but in his celebrated novel *A Rebours*, considered as an early gay masterpiece, edged into 'decadence' and aestheticism and was an inspiration for Oscar Wilde. Subsequently he wrote about Satanism in *Là-bas* and in (un)natural progression ended up in fervent Catholicism.

Two days after this episode, I became so ill on account of the camp's freezing water that I had to be admitted urgently to hospital. After the doctor's visit, I fastened my pack and off I limped, escorted by some corporal or other. I was dragging my leg behind me, sweating beneath my cross-belt. When I reach the hospital I'm turned away; the place is overflowing. Instead I go to one of the nearest field hospitals[2]. There's a bed free, so they let me in. At last I can put down my pack. Before the *major* can order me to stay still, I take myself off for a walk in the little garden that joins up the buildings. Suddenly a man appears from inside, all bristly beard and glassy eyes, burying his hands in the pockets of his long, dark brown cloak. As soon as he's close enough to spot me, he shouts:

"Oi, you! What the hell are you doing?" I go over and explain my reason for being there. He waves his arms about and yells, "Get back inside! You're not to take walks in the garden until you've been given an outfit!"

I return to the ward. A nurse brings me an overcoat, a pair of trousers, a pair of slippers and a hat. I look at myself all bundled up in my little mirror. Good God, what a sight! And what a get-up! With my rheumy eyes, gaunt complexion, short-cropped hair and shining nose, with my big mousey-grey coat, dingy reddish-brown breeches, enormous heelless slippers and huge cotton hat, I look a tremendous state. I can't help but laugh. I turn to face my neighbour in the next bed along: a tall, Jewish-looking chap who's sketching a portrait of me in a notebook. We become friends right away; I tell him to call me Eugène Lejantel and he in turn introduces himself as Francis Émonot. Both of us being acquainted with some artist or other, we start discussing aesthetics and forgetting our misfortunes. Evening comes. We are handed plates of boiled meat specked with a few black lentils and poured brimming cups of *coco clairet*[3]. I undress, overjoyed that I am able to lie down in a bed without keeping my clothes and boots on.

The following morning I'm woken at around six o'clock by a door

---

2 Field hospitals, known as *ambulances* in French, were mobile medical units which followed behind the army in wagons, sometimes constructing temporary buildings, as in this case. 'Hospital', used above, refers to a more permanent building.
3 *Coco* was a drink popular in 19th-century Paris, consisting of water flavoured with lemon juice and liquorice root. Clairet refers to a very light red wine, historically considered to be relatively healthy. Coco clairet would appear to be a mixture of the two.

slamming and voices shouting. I sit up, rub my eyes and see the man from the day before, dressed again in his dark brown greatcoat, approaching imperiously at the head of a procession of nurses. It was the *major*.

Stopping just inside the room, he rolled his dull green eyes from right to left and from left to right, shoved his hands into his pockets and bellowed:

"Number One, show me your leg... your bloody leg. Ah! Not so good, that leg. That wound's gushing like a fountain. Lotion of bran and water, lint, half rations, strong liquorice tea.

Number Two, show me your throat... your bloody throat. Getting worse and worse, that throat, we'll have his tonsils out tomorrow."

"But, doctor..."

"Oh! I'm not asking for your opinion. Say one word and I'll put you on a bloody diet."

"Well, really!"

"Put this man on a bloody diet. Write this down: diet, gargling, strong liquorice tea."

He continued his rounds in this manner, prescribing that strong liquorice tea of his to everyone: venereal patients, the wounded, the fever-struck and the dysentery cases all alike.

Arriving at my bed, he stared at me, tore off my blankets, punched me several times in the stomach, ordered me some egg whites in water and the inevitable tea, then left, sniffing and dragging his feet.

Life was difficult with the people around us. There were twenty-one of us in the ward. On my left was my friend, the painter; on my right was a bugler–a big devil–pockmarked as a sewing thimble and yellow as a glass of bile. He straddled two professions, being a cobbler by day and a pimp by night. Nevertheless, he was a funny chap, who'd stand on his head or on his hands, recounting in the most naïve fashion imaginable the way he'd kick his whores into action, or perhaps singing in his soft tones a sentimental song:

Je n'ai gardé dans mon malheur-heur, Que l'amitié d'une hirondelle![4]

---

4 Refrain of a popular song about a girl locked in a tower: 'A swallow, in my unhappiness, is the only friend I have left.'

an old mistress (from 'une vieille maîtresse')

jules-amédée barbey d'aurevilly

Translated by Tara Isabella Burton

'I plunged myself between her breasts. I hid myself away in her soul, the way the damned plunge their faces into their hands, so that they cannot see God!'

Never previously translated into English, *Une Vieille Maîtresse* appeared in 1866 and was filmed by Catherine Breillat in 2007, with Asia Argento in the title role. Ryno, a young aristocratic Frenchman, has recently married the innocent Hermangarde. But he is unable to resist the call of his magnetic, unstable former mistress, the Spanish courtesan La Vellini, and agrees to visit her once more. In the scene that follows, Vellini sees Ryno for the first time since his marriage.

"Ah! In ten minutes he'll be here!" she cried. Her voice resounded like a trumpet, blown by the proud lips of Victory. She rose, beaming, and took from the chest a crystal platter, patterned in the Eastern style, setting alight a number of small pastilles of amber and of rose from which wafted an intoxicating vapor, which spread throughout the small cottage. Across the snow, she heard the whinnying of a horse, turning between the hedge and the hill. She flung open the door, and between her fingers, gleaming with rings, she hissed out Ryno's name.

He had seen her; he had heard her. He had already emptied the iron brackets and attached to the iron ring, which was in those days affixed to all the gates in Normandy, his sweat-glistening horse, on whose back he had carefully thrown his coat. He came to her, making his way to that frozen threshold where she stretched out her naked arms, her naked face.

"Let's go on in, then. Again this bloody cheek…" he muttered, and entered. The door was closed once more, and they sat together upon the bales of hay. Ryno, trembling with some holy dread – for he felt all too keenly his sin in having stolen by night to this interview, his wife still slumbering in trustful repose – was almost dignified in his melancholy, an aura that only set into relief the sultry sensuality of the *senora* opposite him.

Against the frost he had worn a sable hat – one of Hermangarde's whimsies – and a coat of dull green, cinched at the waist and, like the hat, lined with sable. The tail of the coat, which swayed like the fustanelles of the Greeks, fell to the knee above his creased boots, from which shone steel spurs. Thus outfitted, he had the air of some mysterious alpine hunter, or a chainmail-clad chevalier of eras past. He had all the ripened beauty of a man who has touched upon the greatest intensity of his own power, of his passion, of his deliberation, and who now glides towards the midday-point of his own life, like Helios in his chariot of fire. Vellini took him all in, her gaze luxuriating in his youth.

"Time is as great a fraud as your marriage!" she cried, "As great a fraud as the love which fades and says, "It's all over, forever!" because it fades. But you have come, Ryno! Tonight, we do not have ten years piled high upon our heads – no, you are more beautiful than when I saw you for the first time. The death of our love cannot hold us back, for are we not here, our hands twined like this, ready, perhaps, to call back the past, to start anew our love?"

"Quiet!" he cried. "Just be quiet!" And in his face and in his bearing there was such magnificence that even she, even that capricious and proud Vellini, fell silent.

But after a silence, he spoke again, in the voice of a man long weary of struggle. "Talk, if you want! Say whatever you want to. It's true, after all – I've come. I couldn't resist your letter. I couldn't resist that longing for the past, those sentiments you've awakened in my heart. I tried to snuff it out. I couldn't.

"No fanatic ever threw himself upon his altar the way I've thrown myself at Hermangarde's feet. I've held that charming girl into my arms – as gorgeous as the dawn, as gentle as a king's daughter – held her in my arms like a drowning man holds fast to the raft that saves him. And as God is my witness, it's you – yes, you to whom I've now come – you who have caused all this. You've given her more kisses, more embraces, more caressing tendernesses for her than I ever could have given her as free man. I told you she was beautiful; I feel sure that I love her enough to drown in the very drunkenness she inspires in my heart, and yet... that inevitable sentiment of the pass, this magic that defies all sense, all life, this atrocious mirage that my mind, hypnotized, comes back to again and again.

I plunged myself between her breasts. I hid myself away in her soul, the way the damned plunge their faces into their hands, so that they cannot see God! It's mad – it's in vain! They must see Him! They must feel that burning hand upon their heart. And so it is with me. The past – that which measures and cuts the thread of my life! - has seized hold of the deepest and most visceral part of my being and holds it fast.

"And this, *this*, is why I've come, Vellini. I've heard it said that, in battle, when the breasts of stallions are pierced but lightly by some bayonet, an incomprehensible attraction to pain goads them onwards, so that they thrust themselves upon its point, impaled to the heart. This is the force that has been driving me back to you, Vellini, since the day I saw you again. All our memories were asleep within me, buried beneath Hermangarde's charms, her soft breaths against my chest. And then I saw you. You have dredged up all those entombed thoughts which would, little by little, have disintegrated within my memory and, like a child who sends the plague upon a whole province, simply by stirring the mud from a marsh with his foot, you, with a loveless call from that past live, you have spread the infection from your soul to mine – and poisoned my happiness!"

"I know all that," she said, without emotion. She had laid her head upon his chest, which still shook with the violence of his pain, and when at last the storm had subsided she spoke again. "I know all that," she repeated. "Thus it has been written. We have divided our lives the way men split up a single piece of gold, cut into two so that we each might have a part. But life is not some inert metal." As she spoke she snapped apart her golden comb, and tossed the two halves into the hair, as lightly as if they were but the pieces of a hazel switch.

"Sooner or later, the pieces had to find one another again. The two halves of the heart must join up again, if only to die together in a single, futile twitch. You have fallen victim to the inevitable, because you believed in the happiness Hermangarde could give you, because you believed it could lift you out of the earth and erase your memories.

But remember, Ryno? Did you not see, with me, one day, in the Cevennes, an injured eagle, who carried his wound through the sky, marking in the air the bloody path of his last, tortured flight? Ryno, Ryno, *this* is your story. In Hermangarde's arms, rising to that pure, blue place, you carried within your breast those ten growing years of Vellini, and neither the happiness your wife gives, nor the crown of the heavens, if the eagle I remember had been able to rise up to that crown – can fight again it – not your wound, not his. Oh Ryno – you've fought in vain. And I know you've fought it." An aura of the oracular permeated her gaze, her voice. "My mirror has told me that much. I've seen it all."

And she showed him a little tin glass, hanging from her coral necklace. It was an enchanted mirror, a talisman that had been given to her mother in Malaga by a gypsy on the church steps, as thanks for alms. "You have fought against me, against yourself, against Fate, against blood. The glass has veiled you for a long time. Everything within was hazy, obscured, fogged-up. But now it sees you clearly. Tonight I saw you in it – leaving the great gate of your manor-house in Carteret, coming to me as swiftly as if you had the two wings of an archangel on your shoulders, and your horse the two wings of a hippogriff."

He smiled bitterly at the strangeness of her words, but he knew the truth too well. If she was mad, she was, at least, convinced – and conviction was the force of God, granted a moment in the hands of men. Half-smiling in disbelief – yet nonetheless shaken through by her words – he leaned over to look at the mirror that she held out at the tips of her slender fingers. He saw nothing there but the opaquely green glow of the metal, but as he leaned, his cheek touched hers.

the babel anthology

His flesh knew her flesh. The body, like the soul, has its memories. If the sight of her letters, traced in blood and frozen upon the cold parchment, had first begun to warm his heart, now his blood was no longer dry. It flowed; it coursed through him, burning like carmine, behind all those transparent barricades he had walled up against her.

The galvanizing tremor of cheek touching cheek – it was the spark to the powder!

"I know it all too well," Ryno struggled to speak. "I know too well that I'll regret it tomorrow. That I will take from your side only bleak disgust with myself – but *wherefore art thou, Vellini?*" And already he was looking up at her, losing himself in the vastness of her eyes. Her irises, grown large with the force of her reignited passion, seemed to have absorbed their prey, like a violent blaze which licks the milk from a full cup, and leaves the bottom blackened and charred.

"It isn't me, Ryno – it's Fate! It's blood!" She spoke slowly, stubbornly, blindly, her voice deep and melodic, that she reappeared to Ryno as she had been in the first days of their youth: a mysterious and mythical creature, with shadows in her voice, in her gaze, on her lips, challenging him with these shadows, goading him onwards to nameless pleasures.

This was one of her greatest powers, and to it Ryno had always succumbed. He hoped now that in ceding everything to this irresistible attraction which avenged Vellini her ugliness, plunging himself in, holding nothing back, he would succeed at last in annihilating himself. He was in agony.

He had told himself that his desire was only an illusion of perspective, sensations of the past made grander by their distance, wisps of memory. And he pressed her to his heart with a violent passion, half-convinced he held nothing more than a ghost, convinced that the force of that embrace would make that specter vanish in his arms, and that the charms to which he had fallen victim would at last – at last! - be broken! His thirst grew with his need to slake it.

For Ryno, it was like the story of the Spartans and Helots – the Helots forced to drink in order to deter the Spartans from true drunkenness, but – cruelty of fate! -- in the breast of this accursed happiness, the spell did not break. The phantom was a real and living self, withstanding the madness of his embrace, responding in kind. His drunkenness increased, but he found no satiety in the dregs of his intoxication. The Helot did not deter the Spartan. In vain, with each kiss, each bite, he waited to see his desires fall dead before him, to feel his veins slow, his face cool, his beating breast calm itself at last. But Fate – for so Vellini had prophesied – bitterly betrayed his hopes. The more he plunged himself into that enchanted lake of long-ago caresses, the more he descended into that sea of rapturous agony, the further he found himself from shore – that sandy shore towards which he sought as the end of this guilty pleasure.

He was like that Egyptian priest who longed to prove that long-worshipped Isis was nothing but a fiction, and who tore with one frantic hand her linen strips, her sails. Alas! With each torn sail, he found a miraculous veil, and beneath each ripped veil there appeared again another sail, and the goddess – invisible, always – annihilated any doubt of her mysterious divinity.

alice kahn (extract)

pauline klein

Translated by Sophie Jones

'...not a bad guy, the type you feel you know straight away,
so great is his desire to be discovered.'

Alice Kahn is a beautifully ironic and witty first novel set in a
youthful contemporary Paris where liaisons are facilitated or perhaps
exacerbated by *le net* and actual relationships conditioned by the
ferocious trendiness of boho metropolitan life... This is the the author's
first English publication.

– Anna?

It's a young brown-haired man who asked this. He stopped in front of me. I was sitting on a café terrace, alone, not expecting anyone, well, not at that precise moment, but I caught him in mid-air, just like that, like people catch a stranger at random, to fill a gap.

I lifted my head towards him, and he smiled at me, frozen like a still image, like pausing a film where I'd lost track of what was going on and that, I told myself, thanks to him, it was perhaps time to get back to.

Stood before me, tall as a tallowtree, the man addresses me as if I were Anna, and his entire face is an eager question mark. His eyes beg, asking for something else to happen, to happen here, now, this second, the one when he meets this girl on the terrace, this unexpected moment. He wants me to raise my head, to tell him to stay, that I am Anna, so things can get started.

I don't know either Anna or the young man who has met up with her now, but I see us both in this same setting, me sat on a chair, him stood before me, and we are no less plausible than everyone else. So I cut out this word, 'Anna', from space, and peel it off, as you would with a fruit label. The world around became wallpaper. I didn't move anything forward. I looked at him for a few seconds, his brown-haired look that told me nothing, his dark eyes, his face that signals there's still time to stop seen against the light, the beige strap of his watch which must show the time for our meeting.

"Anna".

– Yes, hello. I reply.

He smiles, I please him.

He takes a breath, pauses, stays still for a moment in front of me, not daring to sit. First he wants to have a look at me. I'm brunette, wearing a pale blue shirt, a man's shirt, and the shorts that I slept in last night. I would never have chosen this outfit, barelegged, like that, for a first meeting. I'm in my pyjamas, like in dreams where you go out forgetting to put your clothes on. And what's more I haven't passed any mirrors. What must I look like? But it would seem to be okay with him.

He smiles, and there is no-one but me. He says "William", and I say "do sit down please". He replies, "we're being all formal then?", and it's my turn to smile.

– I'm sorry, he says, taking the seat next to me. I thought you would have left already. I was into my printing and I really didn't notice the time go by… And then I didn't even have your phone number.

– I didn't notice the time go by either, I reply.

– All the better.

Then the sound cuts off. William seems at ease, as if he's known me forever. He says a few inaudible words, and I watch him exist, express himself, I speed up time as much as possible in order to make this picture in profile familiar: his fidgeting lips, his slender, rather handsome nose, his left eye which appears and disappears beneath an eyelid which claps to say "roll the camera". I enter William's life via his left profile.

How do they know each other, she and him? At a party perhaps, one night. She must be a story from the night before. He met her all made up, in the dark, and me, I'm the follow-up, her morning face, her day face.

Or even over the Internet. He must have matched her expectations, the dark chestnut-brown type, not a bad guy, the type you feel you know straight away, so great is his desire to be discovered. She must have liked this photo of him; he must have posed like he's posing now, on his best day, the image I'm capturing here, and now prolonging.

I make an imaginary ball out of their correspondence. I stick together bits of present moments and fix myself inside them. I'll wedge myself there, for time to discover the track they started together. And I'll pose too to look like that photo. I'd really like to see myself as well, ask him for the photo he must have of me.

I looked straight ahead, drank the last of a coffee I'd already finished drinking a long time ago, and then became shy, my heat beating.

I can see him looking me over from the corner of his eye, my legs, forearms, hair… Myself I act just like Anna's photo, I don't move.

A waiter comes over to take our order. He's our first witness. He asks for a coffee, I order another. That's it, we're in a picture, him and I together around a small, round table, and the others walk past us without thinking anything of it.

Inside this frame, I can move. Look at William's other side, or even at William himself. It's not his decision to appear before me, it's my eye's. And when it opens itself completely, when I dare to let him enter my pupil, his whole body hits me. His beige velvet jacket, a well-chosen pin that's not there for nothing, it says something about art but I can't read what, perfectly scruffy trousers, messy hair, clean hands and shoes that are perfectly designed to look worn.

He seems like anybody else. A canvas, a chicken breast, some modelling clay in a plastic bowl. Above all else, don't frighten him, leave the canvas pristine, the door wide open to all imaginable possibilities.

I give myself an hour. An hour of well-chosen silences, careful trickeries, to make him talk about himself, to glean a few details about myself, or about Anna, to get under the skin of the character.

Afterwards, we'll have to plan another meeting. Outside of this hour, we would leave this ground. The role must be played out in little fragments that he, William, will arrange end to end because that's his name and, once the segments are stuck together, he will make something of me, like one makes a matchstick figure before setting the whole construction on fire.

I seek out what women have in common, the woman behind Anna, a character I will become the mask for, a fragmented portrait, poorly printed, a woman I'll hold like my breath, so that she doesn't get away from me while I wait for him to describe her to me, to provide me my serve.

***

In other people's eyes I am a little abandoned girl. I tell myself that looks wound where they fall on me. I hold them responsible for my injuries, the bruises on my knees, the little scar on my forehead, my collarbone broken at birth.

Nobody sees me. I am always absent, even if I answer at morning register, and the one in the afternoon. When the bell rings, nobody has yet noticed me.

When the time for the class photo comes around, I amuse myself by posing with a class that isn't my own, melting into the group so that nobody finds me on my photo, and nobody looks for me in another.

I hide myself. I play at being invisible for later on. When the moment to impersonate life arrives.

My grades are good or bad. I pass classes without being noticed, I progress, without being noticed. I'm average. I have white skin and keep my eyes down. Sometimes I pull my tights up to just under my breasts in the middle of the school playground, and nobody sees me. Yet my tights are red, and I still suck my two fingers from behind a shapeless cuddly sheep but nobody makes fun of me. Nobody treats me like a big baby. I am not a big baby. I'm invisible to the naked eye. Sometimes I hold the toilet door open, people cut in front of me in the canteen queue, but that's it. Hollow on the inside.

When I was younger, I used to stick my big toe in my father's buttocks, he'd say "stop!", but not move. He ended up turning towards me, and admitting that it tickled. It was a child's game. It was easy for me to explore with my thumb. And then my father left home, before I had had the time to know who he was.

I created a perfect father out of this absence. A great psychiatrist, whose name and surname I invented and looked for on Google until he fitted how I imagined him to be. He had written dozens of books, books on psychoanalysis and a novel too, that hadn't been much discussed but had deserved to be better knwn. One critic had even said that he died too soon, that he wrote about psychiatry like one writes about cinema, and it was true. I started constructing memories with my father, the things he would say to us around the table, his expression, his laugh and the games we'd play together.

I recalled his patients too, from when I stayed home, whose snatches of conversations I would hear and my father's wise words. Faceless patients who would file in and that I would make up stories for.

He had a somewhat dramatic death, a suicide, from medication he had prescribed himself, an overdose. He was found in his office. He had written me a letter that I wrote out myself, and never read to anyone. My father is a hole that I let men through.

***

I live in a two-room apartment, comprising a hall, a living room, a bedroom, a kitchenette and a bathroom, complete with bathtub. There aren't any mirrors in my place. I look at myself in other people's eyes and in all the windows of the world, but not at home.

The apartment overlooks a school playground from where I hear the cries of children in the morning, at half past ten, and at three o'clock. The bell at morning break usually signals the end of my night.

The first room, the one you walk into, is the stage. On the parquet, that I tell myself creaks, a light grey velvet sofa that I've scattered purple cushions on for contrast. On the floor a rug that I call antique, set askew. Opposite, a white wooden table and three black chairs around it, one of which usually remains empty. The window frames are painted grey. The light shines on my feet in the morning, on my breasts in the afternoon.

Outside, white clouds are scattered here and there across a grey-blue sky. The entrance to my bedroom is through a little grey door. My all-white bed is made. A cupboard opens onto some dresses that would make any normal woman die of envy, and a shoe collection, everything that's required. I always dress the same, so as to pass unnoticed. Except that a persona has just been served me on a plate, on my doorstep.

I'll navigate through an image made of possibilities rather than realities. My apartment will become a laboratory to create a girl who gets noticed even when she's in her pyjamas on the side of a deserted road. New and shifting contours will outline my transparency by masking it, and make me visible. I will construct a puppet, an infallible marionette that I will dress up as I go. I will need to prepare. Prepare and rehearse.

I'll become the kind of femme fatale who plucks a man out of the air just to devour him. I'll have new shoulders and a look that speaks a thousand words. I'll invent myself some dreams, the dreams Anna has at night, and that I'll analyse to understand her life.

Other people, chance, the outside world will become my playing field. Like when I decide to find a job. To enter life through the few holes it leaves unguarded.

I'll fill them in like I used to fill in the white space of certain paintings that arrived at the gallery where I had my first job. Because it was necessary to "check in the works" I would add where I could my mark on the surface of the canvas, my fingerprint made with the tip of a black marker. The little holes left to gape by the screenprinting, the black lines that I would go over bit by bit. The invisible holes I used to plug. I'd enter, just like that, into the art community that produced the most expensive works in the world.

I only work when I find the right job taking over a vacant post. The last time it was being a journalist on a magazine. A cultural magazine that promoted exhibitions, books, new artistic trends. I worked on the "top tips" section where I would always slip one or two shows that would never be on or an imaginary exhibition in with the rest.

I used to invent artists too. Amongst these, Alice Kahn often came up. She suited any situation. If the magazine theme was "Immaterial" I would say how Alice Kahn had assumed the author's right to silence.

In an issue entitled "Ephemeral Artists", I would talk about how Alice

Kahn would play golf with an ice cube until it melted. If anyone asked me to talk about the body, a recurrent theme, I would offer them some little performances with electricity, and an exhibition of her injured hands.

Alice Kahn slipped in everywhere, in those places where things were outside the bounds of definition. Alice Kahn's photo was a photo nobody had ever been able to take. An Alice Kahn pain was a diffuse and inexplicable pain. I'd call it an "Alice Kahn stroke" when it started raining when you'd planned to do something outside. An Alice Kahn silence or Alice Kahn luck.

One day a television journalist called the magazine because he wanted to invite this girl onto his show and couldn't find her. I told him the name of her gallery again, but he couldn't contact them. I couldn't do much more for him. I was really sorry.

At the magazine other people started to talk about her too, and to say "Alice Kahn style". Somebody other than me had even quoted her in one of their articles. I was proud of her. I had myself done a telephone interview obtained following a week of negotiation. It wasn't easy.

the babel anthology

daddy leaves/ mummy lies/ granny dies (extract)

fabienne yvert

Translated by C.J. Young

'Daddy wants to go, to see if it's better somewhere else, he
has to find out, he wants to play the Prodigal Son, he's going
to leave at Christmas, the Baby Jesus will take his place,
he's been hearing voices, a friend has invited him to Cuba.
Daddy wants to leave because, because, he's doing the
right thing, he's lost it.'

papa part maman ment mémé meurt (Éditions Attila, Paris 2011) is
by another brand-new author for the Anglo world and if Pauline Klein
is ironic, Fabienne Yvert is sardonic, to say the least, in her dissec-
tion of family life and the interaction of the generations. Her novella,
extracted here, is both enjoyable and delightfully disturbing.

Daddy Leaves

Daddy wants to leave home–why? He's fed up of seeing my mother, he's fed up of green beans, he's sick of coming back to the same place every single night, he's attention-seeking, he wants us to beg him to stay, he can't stand the wallpaper in the living room. I can see his point.

Why does Daddy want to leave home? He hates the cleaning lady, the air is bad for his health, Mummy is a reincarnation of the Virgin Mary, Mummy is a Martian, Mummy was bitten by a vampire, Mummy refuses to do the washing up.

Why does he want to leave? The cat bit Daddy, Daddy wants to eat the cat, Daddy wants to go off with the cat, it's the cat that put the idea in his head, it's a coup staged by the KGB, the cat is a CIA agent, Mummy smells too bad.

Why does Daddy want to leave home? The house is too small for all of us, he's better off elsewhere, he can't stand the smell of my painting, he doesn't like Mummy's hairstyle, he's a hypocrite. He doesn't want to talk, he says he doesn't know, he says he doesn't know how to say it, he says nothing.

He's stupid, he's sick, he's exasperated, he's desperate, he's distant, he's running away, he's been crying, he's got red eyes and a runny nose, he's got a cold.

Why does Daddy want to leave? He says it'll be better this way, he's found somewhere nicer, he wants to be alone with his television, he fancies doing his own cooking, he fancies making eggs for himself, he wants to sleep alone.

Why does Daddy want to leave? He's lost his memory, his health, his happiness, his money, his keys, he can't find them, he won't talk to us about it.

Why does Daddy want to leave? He killed himself this morning because Mummy forced him to stay, he threw himself under a *métro* train because he'd had enough of taking the *métro*, he poisoned us all because he was sick of being poisoned. Daddy wants to go, to see if it's better somewhere else, he has to find out, he wants to play the Prodigal Son, he's going to leave at Christmas, the Baby Jesus will take his place, he's been hearing voices, a friend has invited him to Cuba.

the babel anthology

Daddy wants to leave because, because, he's doing the right thing, he's lost it.

Daddy's going to Saint Helena, he's going to join the Foreign Legion, he's going to rob a bank, he's going to the Moon, Daddy's got AIDS, he's going to conquer Everest, he's going on a round-the-world trip, he's going on a raft, he wants to take a submarine, he wants to fly away, he's been in touch with the Martians, he's going back to his mother's.

Daddy wants to leave home, Daddy wants to be the boss, he wants to be a boy scout, he wants to be single, Daddy wants to become Pope, wants to raise an army, Daddy wants to live in his car, he wants to become a tramp, a martyr, Jesus Christ, God, an outlaw, Jessie James, Zorro, a drug pusher, a singer, a dancer, an acrobat, he wants to become a clown.

Why does Daddy want to leave? He wants to live without a family, without money, without a home, without a job, without the hassle, he wants to become a cobbler, a banker, the wolf and the lamb, Mère Michel and Père Lustucru, vaudeville and Dallas, the stork and the fox, Dumbo the flying elephant, the Ridiculous Preciouses, the Misanthrope, Don Juan, the Miser and the Magic Skin, he wants to be a lowly cripple.

Daddy wants to leave, he's got a letter from Ban Ki-moon, he's got the Nobel Prize, he invented the bomb, he's scared of staying, he wants to die alone, he's putting on an act, scrounging for attention, doing it for kicks, he's got a refined and unusual sense of humour, he's on a quest for the Holy Grail.

He wants to leave, he wants to be a conquistador like Cortès or Pizarro, he wants to discover America like Christopher Columbus, he wants to discover relativity like Einstein, he wants to discover the rabies vaccine like Pasteur or Oceania like Captain Cook, he wants to join the crew of the Bounty with Marlon Brando, he wants to be a rough, tough cowboy like John Wayne, he wants to assassinate Abraham Lincoln like Abraham Lincoln's assassin, he wants to kill Marat in his bathtub with Charlotte Corday, he wants to make an apple fall on Newton's head, he wants to replace one of the Beatles, he wants to vote for French Algeria, he wants to be by the side of Napoleon at Austerlitz, he wants to be the jailer of the Man in the Iron Mask, he wants to cut off Van Gogh's other ear, he wants to write that existence precedes essence before that other guy, he doesn't want to go to Vietnam, he wants to be the fourth of the Three Musketeers, he wants to build the Eiffel Tower in Gustave's place, he wants to paint Mona Lisa's picture, she's an old friend who's been bugging him about it for ages.

Daddy's leaving, he's going to Peru, he's off to Siberia, have you seen DDaddy? Daddy's pretending to go to work, I saw him at the cinema at the four-o'clock show and the six o'clock one, he sings in the corridors of the *métro* with a mate of his who plays the banjo, he shoots up in cars in the supermarket car park, he chews Malabar gum all day long.

Daddy's gone. He killed himself with gas and the house blew up as well, he deliberately put an electric radiator into the bath, he died when the water got too hot, he was all red like he'd been cooked, he ate nothing but soap for a month and the next month he blew bubbles all the time and when he was dead he decided one day he could fly, so he went up on the roof and hurled himself into the flowerboxes, at night he ate his pillow without taking a single drink, he died of indigestion in the early hours.

Where's Daddy? Daddy's gone on a crusade, he's on an oil rig in the North Sea, he's been gathering daisies in Adélie Land, he's taken his bike to Alaska to smoke a cigarette in the Valley of Ten Thousand Smokes, he wants to live on a raft with no radio, he wants to be a scarecrow in the garden, he's completely nuts.

Why's Daddy leaving then? He went off with Mère Denis after seeing the advert on TV, he's gone to fight the war on cancer, he's gone to Ethiopia to give them a bowl of rice, he's gone to Lourdes to perform a miracle, he's at Lourdes trying to cure his mental problems, he's dreamt of going since he was a boy.

Mummy Lies

she's a crazy bitch, she's unbearable, so are we, she wants us to help her do the washing up (with red rubber gloves), she says she doesn't understand what's happening to us, she cries a bit, blows her nose a lot, she says she's just fixing her face when she dries her mascara with a corner of her jumper

but she's only pretending, or at least she's not telling the whole truth. Mummy acts all cool but then chucks the teaspoons down on the table as though she wants them to explode, Mummy acts all hard and mean when really she wants to be kind, she wants us to hug her and comfort her, Mummy criticises Daddy but sort of acts the same way, she's playing a daft game, soon she'll deserve a medal made out of marshmallow

this afternoon she refused to cook for us, she says it serves us right, we rummaged around in the fridge and grilled ourselves some pig's trotters, she'd already eaten the head and she's all wound up like when she spends too long checking if the *apéritifs* are still there, she has little eyes that are sort of holding back the tears, like a dam, her nose is a bit red and she pretends to be looking for her handkerchief when it's always in the same place, she behaves like someone who's trying not to have a breakdown, she does it a bit on purpose to annoy us, she's dead crafty, she's been told she should do amateur dramatics

she says that telly is really stupid but it does her good, she asks if I've got a book I can lend her that you can read without thinking like the Argos catalogue, I tell her I'll go and have a look but actually I don't want to give her any book under these conditions

she's bought herself some girly earrings, she says I've lost weight don't you think? she says she's quite happy, she says are you coming we're off to see a film, she says nothing and just cries

she's on edge, she puts us on edge, she gets on my nerves, she has a nerve, she has pointed teeth, she's spiteful, she's full of anxiety, she's givingg it to us, it's a powerful anxiety, it's not happiness no way

she tells us she feels old, that it's too late to start from scratch, that she just can't imagine it, if she could do it all again she wouldn't, all men are bastards, we don't know what to say

she told us you have to honour your father and mother, she tells us your father is a shit, she taught us you mustn't steal, she says ask your father for some money, she taught us in principle all people, all races, are equal, she says your father's going off with some dirty black whore, she taught us you must forgive, she tells us I'll never forgive him, she taught us animals don't have souls, she calls the cat my baby and she tells us at least he shows her some gratitude, she tells us God helps her, she says her prayers while swallowing down tranquilisers, she says that God is good and Daddy's a pig, I tell her I still prefer Daddy

she tells us Daddy stole her youth, and that I'dstolen the photos of her from when she was happy for my stupid art that's got nothing to do with anything

she deliberately eats without waiting for us, she deliberately scoffs all the bread, she deliberately cooks things we don't like, she deliberately hoovers when we're asleep, she deliberately does the washing when we're having a shower so there won't be any water, she deliberately makes a burnt tart, she deliberately undercooks the green beans, she deliberately drives over the hydrangeas, she deliberately backs into the garage door when she's reversing, she was the one who poisoned the cat but she didn't do it deliberately

she listens in on the phone and when we catch her at it she says she was just about to make a call herself, she listens at doors and when we catch her she says she was just about to walk in, she rifles through our things and when we catch her she says she was just looking for the train timetable, she reads our letters and when we complain she says she didn't notice the name on the envelope and she thought it was for her, in fact nobody ever writes to her and she's hidden the other set of keys to the letterbox behind the radio

she says what do I have left, she says Tara, I still have Tara, she says I'm going back to Tara, she says Rhett, please don't go, you can't leave me, she cries on the stairs she says close the window there's a draught, she says I don't want to go and live in a council flat

Granny Dies

She's thrown up her onion soup all over the bed. It looks like she's slept on a plate of *gratin dauphinois*. She's thrown up the little bit of salad she ate at lunch onto her slippers, it's made little green patterns on them. At lunch today she ate a little jar of baby food, peas and carrots, and afterwards she belched. She was dead. It was her last supper.

Ever since she had the battery put in her heart she's been afraid of a breakdown.

She used to saythe youngsters are on drugs, the English are potty, the Pope has itchy feet, the poor little children over there are dying of hunger, she'd say have some more cake, she'd say is your father better now?

She'd say oh, you've never loved your mother, have you! She'd say will you come and see me in the cemetery? She'd say you look sad, have a cake, she said when will you come again? She said, here you are, here's some honey for the winter.

She really loved Claude François, she really loved granddad, she really loved Pétain, she really loved watching Jacques Martin on the telly on

Sundays, she really loves the numbers and then the letters, she really loved listening to the General on the wireless and Lucien Jeunesse on *Double Your Money*, I'd like to bury her with her old radio and make the worms sing.

Granny died watching night fall. It fell and hit her.

She died in her sleigh bed, it's more practical for getting around in the empyrean. She died in the chicken coop, her soul got feathers stuck all over it and flew away.

sculpture gardens (from 'les jardins statuaires')

jacques abeille

Translated by Sara Helen Binney

'And then I saw it. The object seemed to slip out of the rudimentary form my gaze had at first surrounded it with. Turning it over and over in the sunlight I saw reflections play across it, making a thousand sketches, too fleeting for me to have time to identify, alternately appear and vanish in the thickness of the stone. And yet each shape, even though it eluded me, left me with the nostalgia of some far-off, poignant familiarity.'

'Une langue d'or au service d'un imaginaire poétique' as l'Express put it while le nouvel observateur calls him 'le plus méconnu de nos grands écrivains'.

Even in this short extract Abeille's hypnotic control of language and imagery are perfectly evident. We live in hope some English-language publisher will pick up on this beautiful book.

"These," replied the old man, **"are little statues, being born."** I turned towards him, incredulous. A proud, weary smile slid onto his immobile countenance. He bent down suddenly, grasped a small white shape between thumb and forefinger, pulled it out of the soil and, after getting rid of the brownish film which covered the lower part, he placed it in the hollow of my hand. "Here!" I almost dropped it; its weight, with no correspondence to its volume, let alone its mushroom-like appearance, left me astounded and trembling. And while I turned the thing over between my fingers, I felt a kind of terrible, slow heartbreak spread throughout my being, followed by fear. If the little thing had slipped through my fingers to shatter at my feet (for, remarkably heavy as it was, the object gave the impression of extreme fragility), I would have felt a palpable grief. This sorrow, as we will see, was not spared me. For the whole time I had been examining this object, my companions had been continually observing me. Was I being tested? Did they want to check that they had not been mistaken about me and that I merited the honour they did me? The prolonged, almost inappropriately insistent stare my guide had fixed me with that same morning was slowly clarified in my memory.

"This looks just like a mushroom," I said.

"Look closely," insisted the old man.

And then I saw it. The object seemed to slip out of the rudimentary form my gaze had at first surrounded it with. Turning it over and over in the sunlight I saw reflections play across it, making a thousand sketches, too fleeting for me to have time to identify, alternately appear and vanish in the thickness of the stone. And yet each shape, even though it eluded me, left me with the nostalgia of some far-off, poignant familiarity. I could also sense that my feelings were making a partly evasive move. The fever with which I tried to recognise a definitive image, mixed with the fascination which removed my ability to stop myself at a chosen sight and made me want to hold onto all of them, could easily be caused in part by this strangeness. The fact remained, however, that the marmoreal mushroom I was rolling between my fingers was a real container of virtualities.

"Allow me, sir." Our host took the little statue from my hands. "It is not good to gaze at them for too long in this state." And before I could make any move to stop him, he threw it on a pile of fragments where it smashed like a glass bell. I felt a great pain at this, in my body itself, which started then trembled almost as if the breaking had occurred in my chest and not a few feet away on a bright heap like a pyramid of salt. I was ashamed of having let this brief distress be observed, but my companions looked at me with respect, as if, again, my sentiment was fitting. And I was certainly beginning to dimly perceive that there was some danger in letting oneself be moved by the native statues.

"You see," noted the older man simply.

"Follow me, then," continued my guide, "there are other beds where you will learn about the development of the statues." And so, from place to place, I could examine statues at various stages of development at my leisure. From one stage to another, sketches were appearing, growing, rising, and I could see, in the distance, monumental shapes, immobile and thoughtful, standing at the farthest edge of the land. We passed men pushing carts whose hubs creaked under the weight.

"One of the most important and difficult tasks is to brighten up and transplant, from one flower-bed to another, the statues' bases as and when they grow."

"You therefore need a larger and larger space around each statue, as it progresses?"

"Indeed, but we do not keep all the plants. We have to destroy some of them at each stage, as our dean broke the little shoot you were contemplating to begin with." I turned to the old man.

"That seems to me to be a cruel part of your work." He agreed.

"Perhaps, perhaps, but we must always choose. And we must choose well, know how to recognise the sketch which is worth developing, which has never been seen before, the promise of an exceptional masterpiece. It is impossible to let everything develop fully which is born and strives to grow." And I remained pensive.

"We should add," resumed my guide in turn, "that these fragments are necessary. Ground up again and again until they are nothing more than a very fine powder, they are put back into the ground to grow again. In some places their contours erode the statue as it grows, already giving it form..."

"Make it clear, my dear," interrupted the other man, "that sorts of nebulosities made of little spheres can be seen to form around the rising statues, probably from the object's friction bursting through the earth's pressure, which we know feed the statue as it grows. We have even been able to observe this phenomenon at close quarters; when the tiny sphere has reached a perfect rotundity, it begins to be emptied of its substance which the statue incorporates. And all that is left of it, no longer living, is the stone's skin."

"But," added my guide, "even these last residues are not lost. They crumble in turn and become the earth's colorant as you can see if you look at the fragments which surround us."

I looked around. My eyes, which had for a long time been focused on details requiring my full attention, were dazzled; it was as if we were standing in the centre of the largest, most varied, and most enchanting carpet. Each square of land, from ochre to brown, from grey-blue to metallic green, from ivory to light pink, had its own nuance which bled into the forms which came out of it.

"Yes," murmured the older of the two men, "the stones are the secret eyes of the earth. They contain all the forms and all the colours the earth can create."

We went a few steps further. A group of men were occupied among some young statues.

"Ah!" said my guide, "let's go closer, this will interest you." When we were nearer, I noticed that the gardeners were using hammers and chisels. "They are moving on to the pruning. At each stage of its development the statue puts out disordered buds everywhere. Each time, the final form, towards which it is obscurely developing, is completely up in the air. So we have to constantly recapture it, confirm it, and, to do this, remove in time the extra parts which threaten to make it completely shapeless and monstrous."

And, at that moment, I saw a gardener, with a single, accurately applied tap, detach from a bust an extended finger, an index to judge by its imperative look, which had inconveniently pushed up out of the bridge of the nose. I must admit that confronted by such a stiff finger, which the gardener was putting carefully in a basket much like the ones used by shellfish catchers by the sea, I was momentarily at the mercy of a somewhat mischievous association of ideas, or rather, of forms. Did they sometimes see, springing up out of the ear of a worthy senator, or some other high magistrate in marble, an obscene form clearly distinguished? I did not dare ask my guides. But to close down this question I can tell you now that in the many visits I made to this region afterwards, I never saw anything like that occur, no more than on that first day. Certainly, the human and even animal form flourished in all its nudity and with perfect anatomical correctness. And, having spent enough time with the gardeners to know them quite well, I was sure that they would have considered it shameful, much more than the areas usually designated as such, to hide artificially certain parts of the body on statues which came naked. Still, I never saw sexual organs grow where they weren't expected, but on the contrary always in the right place, as if they really were the most regular, most necessary, most inevitable things, while all around the most misplaced forms multiplied on fanciful chance's whim.

"But," I then asked, "when is the statue's definitive form finalised? Because it could become many things, and you probably have to start very early in order to establish a regular shape." And I gestured to an incredible confusion of body parts in front of us. "And if so, a gardener must be a very sharp observer to find the lost form when it is covered in such a profusion of outgrowths."

My guide smiled at me. "But that is not exactly how we work. Did I not tell you that the statue was completely up in the air at each stage of its development? I realise I was not precise enough. This is what happens. From the first transplanting, when the statues have reached a slightly more evolved state than the bud you first looked at, they are already showing sketches of forms. That is when we carry out the first pruning. The gardeners clarify the form they think they see sketching itself out. Each one, tools in hand, trims some feet, but there are never two working on the same statue. At the next transplanting, the same operation is repeated, but the gardeners choose the statues they prune by chance. And even if, still only by chance, the same man encountered a single statue on two occasions, he would have been involved in much other work in the meantime, during which the stone could have entirely changed its appearance. The man's inspiration takes a new direction each time while the statue can completely overturn the plan of its evolution."

"I was amused one day," the old man told us, "to notice a foot. I was not involved in the pruning of this foot, but I was taking great care over its transplanting. So I was able to watch what at first was becoming an equestrian statue of some general finally end up representing the softly languid body of a nymph, her arm lying across an urn. I will leave you to imagine the tremendous series of metamorphoses it must go through in order to change from a warlike, and, what is more, equestrian statue to a calm and sensuous woman's body." He nodded. "In fact, the initial stone is an egg which conceals an infinite number of possibilities."

"And yet," added my guide, "we have to admit there is a certain continuity of temperament among the gardeners, which means that each estate is marked by a style so particular that the statues which come out of it cannot be confused with any other."

"It has to be that way," added the other man, "because we all know the stone is blindly searching for its form. We all have the impression that it makes us the gift of its potential, our task is to prove ourselves worthy of it."

I began to vaguely discern a necessary link between an apparently austere morality, which allowed me to foretell the remarks which had just been made to me, and the fierce demand to keep the field of possibilities free and open. But since I was contemplating these ideas in their concrete and even palpable state, as it were, I did not dwell on my speculations. "Why," I asked, "do you keep some fragments so carefully, that the gardeners are putting in their baskets? Is all that not destined to be broken to prepare the soil that you told me about?"

"You are mistaken," said my guide. "We only break the statue seedlings that we have definitely given up on.

"What you see here are our cuttings, because we must prepare for new statue seedlings. Long tradition has taught us that the parts which lend themselves best to the reproduction of statues are certain modestly-sized parts which reach a state of perfect completion, but have to be removed from the form as a whole because they break its harmony. The smaller these parts are, the more impeccable their form is, the better the seedling will be. So at the moment you can see our gardeners retrieving all these ears, all these fingers, all these toes, these noses, these nipples, even; they put them in the baskets arranged at their feet. Very soon, they will take them to the greenhouses where they are sorted so that only the best elements are conserved. These will be potted for a few weeks in the dark. There, they will lose their individual character to uniformly take on that mushroom-like appearance that you saw."

"In this way," the old man added, "we can, starting with any fragment, recreate a complete statue. The initial piece's form in no way determines the evolution or the final form of the statue to which it will give birth, no more than the place it was taken from."

The gardeners, now that they had finished pruning all the figures in the flower-bed, took damp scraps of fabric from large wooden buckets and applied them to the places which had just been cut, although it seemed to me that no trace of it could be detected on the stone. I asked what this new operation was.

"It is a necessary precaution," my guide explained. "If we do not do

the babel anthology

this, we risk seeing the statue, a few weeks after its completion, suffer from an incurable plague."

"It is strange, this disease of the stone," added our host. "At first it is only a single point, a bluish trace like a light, miniscule bruise, still somewhat indistinct, which little by little enlarges and hollows out in a geometrical progression, forming a crater from which a sterile powder falls, and all that remains of the statue is a rough skin which flakes off. Only then is the stone really dead."

"And the damage is incurable. We have tried to scrape off the diseased part, to result in smaller dimensions a new statue inside the old one, while it is only superficially affected. We have attempted amputation. We have even endeavoured to pull out the parts of little statuettes which are apparently still healthy. Nothing works; sooner or later, in the smallest fragment, the plague reappears and succeeds in causing death."

"And the disease is contagious, it spreads to those close by. It can damage a whole farm if immediate precautions are not taken. As soon as a statue is affected, it must be placed in a wagon, covered in branches and removed as fast as possible towards the end destiny has assigned to it. It is a long journey to the outskirts of the country, to the abyss. We have an establishment there." The old man fell silent for a moment. He stared pensively at the ground without seeing it. I turned to my guide to ask him for some more details concerning the sad undertaking which had just been described. He was standing still, arms crossed, apparently deep in thought. I did not dare distract him. Following the example of the two men accompanying me, I stayed quiet, thinking of what I had just learned, imagining, far from all human labour, this place which I envisioned as desolate, at the edge of the country: an abyss. My thoughts swirled like wreckage around this image. The old gardener's voice pulled me from the reverie I was sinking into…

"Let us imagine that, during pruning, this protection proves ineffective. Sooner or later we will have a diseased statue. The disease only appears when the statue is complete and, fortunately, it is only then that it becomes contagious. When one of the gardeners, while working on statues which have reached the last stage of their development, discovers a suspicious spot on one of them, he must warn the dean of the farm straight away."

"Here, I am the dean," explained the older of the two men. "They inform me that the disease has appeared on our land, I must immediately divide the gardeners into two teams. The first and largest has the job of moving all the ancestors' statues, which are in the house. Under my direction, the men put these statues on carts; we hasten across the farm and line the statues up along the periphery wall, outside, on the pavement, on both sides of the entrance. This sign tells all our neighbours of the misfortune we are suffering. This done, we return to the house. For us, a period of fasting and of silence begins which will last until the other team returns.

"The second group of men, meanwhile, load the diseased statue onto a wagon. They have completely covered it with freshly-cut branches. They cross the estate, go through the door that the other team left open and make their way as quickly as possible towards the abyss. It takes them several days and great exertion to reach it.

"Once there, they hurl the statue into the depths of the earth. For a long time they remain motionless, breathless on the edge of the abyss, still hearing in their minds the echo of the statue bounding from one of the slope's protrusions to another, shattering on the overhanging rocks and scattering the loose stones. No-one knows the depth the statue's scattered limbs reach before they crumble. After this, the wagon must be burned."

The dean told me of the rest of the ceremony which takes place under the warden's authority. I learned of the gardeners' wait, carrying their exhaustion and their grief like an offering, pierced with sorrow, lined up against the house waiting to be recognised, the construction of the pyre at the edge of the abyss, the wagon in the pile of firewood, the tall flames' crackling which tore into a slow twilight, the pit of ashes where the rising night wind made pale streaks, the men's ablutions in the washing-place where the mountain water runs over slate slabs, the cleansing of the cattle by the warden who ritually sprinkles them down in the pool, the sleep of beasts and men, the utter darkness.

the babel anthology

ballast (from 'ballast')

jean-jacques bonvin

Translated by Calypso Blaj

'In the pockets of these wool coats on 42nd street, with their honey and sottobosco-coloured dogtooth pattern, can be found some pill-bottles and sachets, wisps of tobacco, a few small forgotten joints, keys for who knows what doors, dimes and pencil butts and the tiny plans for long novels sketched out on squared paper.'

Bonvin's piece, in another book from the fertile presses of *Éditions Allia*, deals in a paced kind of prose with the 'four musketeers' of the Beat Generation...

Day and night for weeks on end they would trail from park to park, from Central to Battery, with LuAnne in the lead, all together in the city where the best possible times of their life were reaching their close.

While the four of them run down 8th Avenue taking up the whole sidewalk, a few blocks away Dylan Thomas is getting ready to meet some journalists. He still has six days before the press conference, six days of drinking, obviously. With three days remaining he manages to break his own record. The record is broken, but at the expense of his liver. On the ninth of November 1953 he collapses in the White Horse after having drunk a still unquantified number of whiskies, and, as is right and proper, was taken to St Vincent's Hospital. Just a few paces away, with a few roads to cross before reaching the great hall beyond which everything may be seen. He was thirty-nine when he died. Pneumonia was diagnosed, as well as liver failure and intracranial hypertension as an *aggravating symptom*. This jargon will one day be pronounced for Jack and Neal, as well as Allen. That omnipresent liver that Lowry, born like Thomas on the fringes of Britain, also overworked. But Lowry's time will be four years later. The group that is currently on 42nd street, coats against the wind, will manage to live well into the sixties, or even longer.

In the pockets of these wool coats on 42nd street, with their honey and sottobosco-coloured dogtooth pattern, can be found some pill-bottles and sachets, wisps of tobacco, a few small forgotten joints, keys for who knows what doors, dimes and pencil butts and the tiny plans for long novels sketched out on squared paper.

Establishing a connection of cause and effect between the liver and the pencil which outlined the traces on these pieces of paper is impossible, and, in fact, irrelevant. If the liver-damaged write at their best on whatever scraps of paper they find, it's clear that it is possible to do the same with all organs intact: with nothing ailing the lungs, liver, stomach, pancreas etc. But by the same token, a healthy writing body will also deliver a last tribute to the medical profession at the moment of death. Neal, LuAnne, Jack and Allen were smiling. They are what they will become, only in better health.

The evening sun was shining onto the solid brickwork, the crumbling render and the windows, as their shadow was diagonally split in two. The foyers of the cinema were gloomy places, smelling of velvet and predation, of love and murder both, one goes in so as not to remain an urban virgin, A cosmos, of Manhattan the son, Turbulent, fleshy, sensual, eating, drinking and breeding. At least Whitman had a working liver right to the end and he designed his own tomb.

Hand in hand the four of them head south, to the Village and the White Horse, which they enter, fists in the air and screeching with joy. Jack talks to the woman serving beer and whisky at the bar, situated directly opposite the entrance, and introduces her to Neal. He turns to Allen and LuAnne for confirmation. He's not far off delirium, all those bars between the park and here, a mild delirium if you will. He knows. He leaves stumbling in total disarray but wakes up with a reasonably clear head. Only his liver suffered. It was Neal's fault, he'd come in from Frisco and offered to buy a round. They had the habit of causing a ruckus as soon as they got to the White Horse, but there was something worrying, like the tale of a suicide, in Neal's look as he nodded his head. His face and his profile too were gentle but the same could not be said for his eyes. They shone out from a place that the most hardened barmen recognised as a lot of trouble on the way.

[...]

They sit down. Jack gets up, leans across the bar and raises his glass. He toasts LuAnne first, then Allen and Neal. Neal is the greatest, Jack says. He's stolen 333 cars and read Finnegan's Wake, he'll write the Great American Novel in 666 days, it'll have 999 pages. Jack Kerouac would do the preface. Allen puts his hand on his shoulder and tells him to quieten down. A waitress behind the bar is on the verge of collapse. Neal's look and Jack's voice are merging in her head, one sets off the other. It's going to get out of hand if Jack doesn't calm down, and fifteen minutes later it does. Two men come out of the kitchen and throw them into the street, starting with Allen who is furious. He tried to keep a lid on things. Neal and Jack came afterwards. LuAnne is *invited* to join them. She downs her glass and leaves, goes back and gives the finger to the crying waitress. The other three wait for her on the pavement, hug her in their arms and sing at the top of their voices, looking up at the stars starting to appear and the orange windows of Hudson Street.

the babel anthology

schasslamitt (from 'schasslamitt et autres contes palpitants')

bérengère cournut

Translated by Jennifer Tennant

'Albertine stands naked against the garden wall, deep in contemplation. It is early in the night. She is twenty.'

Bérengère ('Beri-Beri' to her *amis*) asked us to tell you this: 'Bérengère Cournut has been writing in a state of paradoxical wakefulness for about ten years. Her texts are longer or shorter depending on the length of the days.' So now you know. Anyway, we think her work, translated with love by Jennifer Tennant, is original, interesting and amusing – and we wish people were writing like this in English instead of the pompous turgidity or vacuous and repetitive triviality of our prize-winning authors (Yawn McEwan? Notanothermanchester-jewishfarrago Jacobson? Hilary Oneforthemantelpiece?) and all the other 3-for-2ers. (Hint: if you are *get in touch*.)

Albertine

Albertine stands naked against the garden wall, deep in contemplation. It is early in the night. She is twenty.

Albertine was born more or less in chime with her century, on 4th April 1901. A nimble-handed pair – a chair caner and a weaver –, her parents, Ulrich and Eugénie Bouleau, lived in a village called La Rivière, not far from Chartres. Albertine was the joyful new existence they had been awaiting for years: spending their days spinning, weaving, winding, mingling their threads and their canes, and with them their love, there had until then been no space left between them for any being – no matter how small. It was said in the village that those two would never produce anything apart from the goods they crafted, and Ulrich and Eugénie had started to believe this themselves when, one morning, Eugénie knew for sure that she was pregnant. She kept the news to herself the whole day, then, as soon as he got home, she told Ulrich. Who locked the door behind him: they would stay where they were until the child was born.

Months went by. To those who came by to make worried inquiries, they replied from behind the shutters: 'We're fine! Go away. There's a surprise coming.' Nobody in those parts believed that the surprise could be a baby: since when had it been necessary to shut yourself up like that? Rather, they imagined that Ulrich the chair caner and Eugénie the weaver were preparing something spectacular for the Spring Fête. But the weeks went by, and the Spring Fête with them. The young couple had still not emerged.

Inside their den, Ulrich and Eugénie caned and weaved away solidly day and night, but in doing so they had only one purpose in mind: optimal incubation of the baby. Ulrich's chief fear was that the baby would come out too soon. In the very earliest weeks he had made for his wife's stomach a wicker girdle that he refashioned every night, believing the little one to be asleep at that time and therefore not growing. During the day the couple stayed in bed; Ulrich held Eugénie very tight.

The child, the future Albertine, might have taken all this very badly – might have sworn that they were put out by her getting bigger, might not even have survived the restraining contraption. But instead she developed a great resilience to all trials, a characteristic that made of her a hard, intense – phenomenal – little bundle. Without knowing it, her parents were creating an emotional force of nature.

The end of the year and the beginning of winter arrived. Relieved that they had so far managed to hold onto the child, Ulrich and Eugénie loosened their grip. Albertine did not catch on straightaway and had them waiting some few long weeks before deciding to leave her mother's stomach. When she did finally put in an appearance, her father, drunk with joy, welcomed her head with both hands, deeply touched to be holding for the first time his best ever piece of workmanship – for it has to be said that the child was extremely pretty. Next came the arms: tense, eager to squeeze something or someone as soon as possible. Then at last Albertine was fully born, detaching herself from her father only in order to wind herself around her mother. All three remained suspended in the happiness of that bedroom for several more weeks.

Then it was decided that they would venture outside. Eugénie dressed Albertine, Ulrich opened the door, and together they went out, enveloped in one enormous scarf. The inhabitants of La Rivière did not realize at first what had happened to the Bouleaus: what could they possibly have conjured up since they had last been seen that they couldn't even walk about outside without huddling up against each other and bawling like that? But eventually the villagers noticed the little head poking out from between Ulrich and Eugénie. Immediately everybody was rejoicing. They had waited so long for this child and now they all wanted to touch her. Albertine inspired a delirious love.

She spent the first years of her life sailing between one set of arms and the next, bouncing on every set of knees in the village. Naturally self-confident, she would walk into any house in the village, where her playful, entrancing little ways prevailed over whatever activities were taking place: washing, sharpening, eating all stopped so that everyone could hug the irresistible intruder. Everywhere she went she was treated like a little queen.

Then, one day, a circus set up not far from La Rivière. Drawn by the bright colours of the big tent, Albertine crossed the boundaries of the world where she was so well known. Suddenly life took on a whole other aspect. Her entry, discretely operated via a raised flap of canvas, did not interrupt the artists at work. A pair of contortionists were busy training. Believing them to be victims of protracted embracing, Albertine was interested; she sat herself down in the amphitheatre to see how they would get themselves out of their fix. They were in a far-gone state of dislocation when a different sound caught her attention: not far from where she was sitting, on the same bench, something red was giving off noise and water, and coughing like a storm. Albertine moved closer: it was a little boy in tears.

As someone who had been treated very generously by life up until then – and a good thing too, at four years old –, Albertine was fascinated by such anguish and decided to ask the little boy some questions. His name was Pierre, he was nine, and he was crying because 'Chekhov' – no doubt his dog – had died. Delighted to hear all this, Albertine applauded with both hands and gave Pierre a kiss. At this the little boy found himself miraculously consoled and invited Albertine to take a turn with him outside. Forgetting all about the contortionists, Albertine accepted, and from that day on she did not let Pierre out of her sight. For months on end she trailed after him everywhere on her tiny legs, even found her way into his home, and accompanied him on his travels. Her secret hope was to see the astonishing geyser of tears spout forth once more. But this was not forthcoming. For the most part, Pierre was content to spend his time whinging and sinking himself in a bucket of black ashes. One day, having fallen into an especially deep hole, he even wanted to free himself of Albertine and send her back to her parents. But she held strong…that is, until he shut himself up in his bedroom definitively. Albertine had no choice but to return to La Rivière.

At this point life could have taken up again as it had left off, between one set of arms and the next, but Albertine had lost her appetite for such things…Just imagine going back to that, after associating all this time with a big boy almost two years bigger than herself! She had come to know life, anguish and boredom.

By then Pierre was a gifted writer. Although she could not see him anymore, she often went and stood against the wall of his house in order to feel the tremors of his quill coming from deep down in the foundations of the building. In the morning, Pierre's parents would find her at the end of the garden, naked and fast asleep. What was to be done about this young girl?

Tonight Albertine is twenty. She thinks back to the tears of her Pierre and to the silent years she spent by his side. Now the time has come to forget him. A strong pair of arms are waiting for her in La Rivière, a pair of arms for which she would like to recover her powerful charms.

The wall against which she has been leaning for so long trembles slightly. It begins to sweat, and to sweat, so much that it forms a sea at the feet of Albertine: and that is the last that ever there was of Pierre the writer, who otherwise left behind just a few texts, all of them scanty – and unending.

the babel anthology

Melanie...or Henrietta?

00:00 hours, in red digits. It is comfortably warm. Something is sticking into my stomach a bit, but if I change position the pain shifts, then softens.

The smell is quite strong in here. Not necessarily bad, though.

I definitely shouldn't have woken up – it's still night time. But I don't feel like sleeping. If I close my eyes, it's not the mists of sleep that overcome me, it's the mists of something else, which I know well. And they don't send you to sleep. Why force things?

I turn what must be my neck – it seems to be quite supple –, and between the disjointed planks of the roof over my head, I can see the halo of a half-moon. The hours go by, it seems, and yet I never tire of gazing at this sight. The light drifts with infinite slowness, filtering more or less weakly through the roof of the shelter. I say 'shelter' because I haven't yet established its exact nature... I have no memory of it at all. But then, strictly speaking, do I even have any memories? With great difficulty, I try to remember my name: Melanie, maybe. Or Henrietta? It's definitely one of the two. I need to have established at least that by morning.

Anyway, my armpits are certainly warm enough! It's not that I can really feel my arms all that much, and I don't really know what to do with them, but it's very hot down there... The other thing is, I can *see* – and very well, at that. I see very roundly, very sharply, very clearly. Not so pleased with my hearing, on the other hand. I can make out a vague murmuring, some rubbing sounds, perhaps – nothing very distinct. But then, is there really anything to hear?

Ah! Here are the first rays of dawn. All around me, masses of others are all a-flap and waddling about. Indeed my own body begins to shake with strange spasms just as, about a metre away, a cockerel appears, screeching. The door of the shelter opens, a hand is placed on top of the meter with the red digits, and a still half-asleep farmer appears, a bucket of grain in one hand. Lifting myself up on my claws, I notice an egg.

I'm a chicken and it's Sunday.

Ciboulette and Ciboulot

This year in the republic of N., Easter Monday, whether by chance or necessity, has fallen on the commemoration of the massacre of Saint Elk of the Empty Woodland, a day itself decreed by the President as set aside for national mourning in memory of a famous musician freshly deceased (though admittedly after twenty-six years of aphasia). In other words, nothing is open in town.

Ciboulette is sitting at home in her lounge, staring into space. A fire, lit more than anything to fill the silence of that morning, crackles in the hearth.

'Tell me, Ciboulet [that's her husband], did you think to buy some fresh fingers?'

'Ah no, that…you're right. And everything's closed today. It's silly of me, I should have used the day off work to put the holes in the wall.'

For several months now, the big DIY stores in the republic of N. have been running their fresh finger campaign: 'For a hold as sure as your own two hands!' The principle is very simple: the fresher the finger, the straighter it is, and the more easily it can be pushed into the wall. As it corpsifies, it contracts behind the wall on which this or that object has been hung. The job is guaranteed for twenty years.

But not twenty years starting from today, Easter Monday and the commemoration of Saint Elk of the Empty Woodland etc., because Ciboulot has forgotten.

The fire goes on crackling, upsetting the birds nested in the chimney. And there we were, thinking spring had arrived! Spring is all well and good, but that morning…

'It's been two years since we last kissed,' cries Ciboulette all of a sudden, without taking her eyes off the rug.

Her husband gets up with difficulty – nothing hurts, there is no pain at all, but the slightest exertion is always a great effort –, moves over to his wife's armchair, grasps her by the shoulders and plants a kiss on her forehead: 'There you are! And just because I don't do it often doesn't mean that I don't love you.'

Here they are again now, as before, one opposite the other, planted firmly in their armchairs. There's still no noise outside, nobody has walked passed the window. There is nothing to be seen but the faint shadow of their bodies, dancing on the wall at the back of the room.

Ciboulette has shifted her gaze to the rug's central motif.

'I'm going to put the radio on.' Ciboulot reaches his hand towards the stand and presses the button. Clic, krcchh, krcchh. Can't hear the usual jingle. He turns the knob a little.

On hearing the sound that splurts out of the radio, Ciboulette sits up straighter and stiffens: it's the rattle-like voice of the woman next door. 'But you know, André. André. André. In today's society, André. André. In today's society there are the nice people and then there are the scoundrels. André. André. What you're doing is a waste of time, André. Listen to me, André. André? Do you know what you're doing, André? You're eating the cakes I sent you. André. André-andré-andré. It's not real life, that, if you jump over the fence, André!' Clic. The radio is switched off.

'She'll have bought herself a new phone. A wireless.' Ciboulot raises his eyebrows, and is reassured to see Ciboulette relax.

Nearly midday. The three little balancing balls of the glass-domed clock on the mantelpiece complete their last circuit before the twelve strikes begin. Ciboulette gets up: 'Right. I'm going to lay out the bricks. They should be dry by now.'

Schasslamitt

'That cat, that cat!' my uncle was always saying. 'What to do about that cat? Hopeless!' And he would jealously fondle his dog, which was always huddled up idiotically against his legs at the end of the table.

It's true that we didn't draw what you could call a huge benefit from the cat's being there, but then what do you expect? He promenaded his thick tail over all the furniture, disturbing the balls of dust like herds of scattering sheep and depositing in their place tufts of even more volatile hairy matter. His passage over the kitchen sideboard – always conducted at the sacred hour of family mealtimes – was always a tense moment. Auntie would lower her head, and my uncle would chew away nervously, following the cat's progress among the ornaments with a sinister eye.

My sister and I witnessed this mysterious unease with incredulity. But not daring to side openly with the cat, we had to content ourselves with a shrug of the shoulders. He was a cat, and that's all there was to it. If we had all just let him be, the atmosphere during the holiday would have been considerably lightened as a result. As far as my uncle was concerned, however, there was no question of this ever happening. So we said nothing, apparently busy lapping up every last bit of soup from our bowls.

When the cat conveyed his majestic presence into the upstairs bedroom my sister and I shared, we did our best to forget all that about our uncle and his stinking dog, our stupid aunt, and the boredom of mealtimes. If a moth came out of the wardrobe, we would immediately both start yelling in unison: 'After the moth! After the moth!' Sitting there on his ass, the cat would watch our excitement, completely indifferent. 'Couldn't he make a bit of an effort too?' And, tired of trying, we would squash the insect with an old shoe.

One day my sister was given a bra as a present for her tenth birthday – 'But I don't have any titties!' – and we decided to use it to make a garment for the cat. It was summer. The sun came in through the window, biting at the bed on which we were sitting. The bra was striped pink and white with green polka dots. Abhorrent. Based on the size of the cat, we agreed a bonnet would be best. When carefully positioned, the fabric end seemed to have been made specially to fit his head and the straps cut to just the right length to tie the bow.

Overpowered by my sister's small but firm hands, the cat found himself assuming the headpiece. Of the two ears, only one was unable to straighten out correctly from under the hat. We engineered a hole; now it was perfect.

Schasslamitt carried out his role as our delegated jester most honourably during the few minutes that his torture lasted. Spitting, walking backwards, one paw then the other reaching behind his head, he struggled hilariously, and to our great enjoyment. But finally he found salvation against the corner of a piece of furniture.

We spent the rest of the afternoon looking at the bonnet lying abandoned on the floor. The cat had made off, and the bedroom was sad again.

We were pleased to see him re-emerge at dinnertime, and this was no doubt apparent from our faces. Sickened, my uncle set his masticatory mechanism reeling with tenfold force, whilst my aunt upped her nodding duncery to the same degree. Coming on top of the fortnight we had just endured, this was too much. Really! Schasslamitt was literally the only thing worth anything in this wretched back of beyond, and now they expected us to sit by and watch them scoff at his spectacular survival!

We only needed to exchange a single glance. My sister ducked under the table and grabbed the mutt that was snoring stupidly at our uncle's feet. She put it down on the table next to the cold meat à la mayonnaise. I grabbed the meat knife that was lying in front of Auntie's glass and, not batting an eyelid, I stabbed. The blood streamed onto the plastic-coated tablecloth.

Uncle sat there with his mouth open some long while before collapsing under the table. Heart attack. That was the last time we holidayed in the Dordogne.

Thaddeus and Uriana

Two beings not known and not able to know one another.

Thaddeus is the enigma behind this wide profile, slipped into every interstice of the nonetheless slight and already full Uriana. Nature had carefully ensured that they were separated by births temporally and racially far-flung, but today, alas, they intermingle and become tied in a touching manner.

Thaddeus was initially an austere, massive figure, at war with the elements, offering no foothold, ever. Resistant to wind and water, he passed through the ages intact, not hesitating to slip into flight when infiltration threatened. But, believe it or not, one can always find craftier than one's sworn enemy.

It is during a walk in the future of death one day that Uriana discovers his unique relief. He seemed then perfectly virgin, which allowed her to form an idea in advance of his difficulty or his unexplored nature. It would have been enough to kindle anybody's curiosity. And Uriana did not lack curiosity.

The mountain appeared before her like a step towards the skies. She lingered around him for a while, hesitant, asking herself whether she did not perhaps risk an irremediable fall. Impassive, the mountain seemed to be sleeping. Uriana was at that time an innocent little weasel with a discrete, but inquisitive mind; she decided to nestle down here for a while, to wait and see.

A century went by, in the space of which she underwent several metamorphoses. Passing indifferently from the form of a rodent to that of a stream, she discovered in the latter, finally, a carefree, pleasant life. The summit of the mountain would sometimes disappear in the mist, would send down a horse or an avalanche that she would watch go by, enthusiastic or perplexed, but never dwelling on any of it.

One day, however, no less than one whole side of the mountain collapsed. For several days, the only sound to be heard was that of rolling rocks. Then, when all was clear and the mountain was once again silent, Uriana contemplated the extent of the damage. Devastation; the universe free of all worry. The moment of ascension, perhaps, had arrived.

The funny thing was that the summit had disappeared, replaced by a name, Thaddeus, filling up the whole of the visible horizon. A few letters, as arduous as they were ardent, extremely difficult – a muddle thick as magma. And worlds away, incomprehensible, some images: a train on top of an enormous strawberry, a hamster weaving between the spokes of a bicycle wheel, a little monk restraining his need to piss with a pair of tongs for picking up flint, a bather suspended under a bridge notorious for suicides, a car turned upside down on the roof of a Polish opera house, a piece of bronze as bare and high as an athlete's buttock, handfuls of dispersed flesh and, and, and...a miniscule marmot who mocked the surrounding din with little whistling sounds.

After four or five centuries of such somersaulting (one night, perhaps?) – a return to calm, a return to reality. A small apartment. Thaddeus is a man. But for how long? He has transformed Uriana into a lounge rug. She is never out of his sight. The opposite is also true, perhaps. What could possibly have happened? How long have we been here? Painfully they crawl, back to back, towards a world of the time of mountain and weasel. Her liberty has got caught up in the branches of his tranquillity; it's a tangle of contradictions and the unnatural, itself suffocating inside a membrane of lukewarm happiness. When, trying to convince herself, she wants to say: 'Let's forget about all that, it's too cruel', she finds herself out of breath, noisily inhales the end, fails to become a pig, falls silent. Reflects a moment: could this mean the end of the age of metamorphoses? One more second: but in that case, what is this the age of? Thaddeus: 'Are you joking?'

Huddled up in the grip of the octopus, the weasel bestows her caresses. And awaits the next metamorphosis.

the babel anthology

love in the balance (extract from 'l'amour en équilibre')

bertrand guilbert

Translated by Valerie Worth-Stylianou

'A happy band took the path through the woods towards
the meadow, singing wedding songs.'

And now for something rather different, a provincial-set tale haunted by a relatively recent but now unimaginable past: the German occupation of France. *Love in the Balance* is the translation of Bertrand Guilbert's *L'Amour en équilibre* (2011). Guilbert has published several story collections and another novel in French, but this is the first English translation of his work, done by Valerie Worth-Stylianou, former Professor of French at Exeter University. Copies of the elegantly produced French published English translation are available via *tba* (post free, email ray.keenoy@gmail.com pay by paypal) or at the Albion Beatnik Bookstore in Oxford, £9.99.

From **Part 1: Stormy Weather Autumn 2007**

Since Monday the wind had been playing in the treetops. The poplars were swaying in the clouds, nodding to the countryside; gusts plagued the apple-trees relentlessly.

At the end of the week, the wind inhaled the air from the valley, puffed out its cheeks and spat it out over the orchard.

The apples crashed heavily to the ground, bumping against each other and forming a pulp which only the cows would want to eat after the storm had passed.

The roots beneath the ground clung firmly to the clayey Normandy soil.

I knew that some old trunks would not be able to withstand the pressure. The first to give way was the apple tree, near the watering trough; it was split right down the middle, where a parasitic mushroom had chosen to dwell.

From the bay window of my house, I watched the violence being unleashed.

The oak by the edge of the vegetable bed fell like a pawn, with a crashing of broken branches. It tore open the earth, and a crater appeared at the foot of the fallen trunk; a sense of death crept over the countryside, and a shiver ran down my spine.

The whirlwind stopped for a moment, then started up again before stealing away, ashamed of having killed a giant. A tear ran down my cheek.

I decided to wait until the morning to inspect the damage.

Dreams coursed through my mind that night: trees trembled under the martial blows of thunder, they huddled close together like frightened children.

The old tomcat woke me up as his rough tongue licked my cheek, then the foul smell of his breath sent me diving under the covers. I went back and forth between the bed and the bathroom, re-reading what I'd written recently, making some corrections.

The fear of discovering the damage wrought by the storm confined me to my room. At around ten o'clock, my stomach insisted that action was needed.

I opened the front door, a slice of bread and butter in my left hand and a precariously balanced cup of tea in my right. I was afraid I would find a scene of desolation.

Only two trees had fallen onto the grass. I felt calmer, my anguish subsided. I walked around the oak, paying it my last respects, those of a friend. It was at that moment that my foot struck a large stone which had undoubtedly been brought to the surface when the tree was uprooted.

I took a shovel from the garden shed so that I could extract the stone and use it to decorate one of the flowerbeds. The earth around the slab was unlike that on the rest of the land, it was blacker. The soil must have been brought here from somewhere else. Once I had cleaned the enormous stone, I realized it was not the only one. I prodded the ground with an iron bar. What traces of the past could possibly be hidden there?

To prevent the cows – who are the most curious of animals - from disturbing my archaeological labours, I set up an electric fence around this area.

They are always ready to oblige, dropping clods of manure here and there to give the place a distinctive smell.

I filled my wheelbarrow with the rich soil, a handful in each hand, and pushed the old contraption, all three feet and one wheel of it, towards the vegetable garden, where I emptied the contents at the bases of the raspberry canes.

After several journeys back and forth, I began to feel as though my arms were growing longer under the weight of the loads. I had a fleeting image of a gorilla which can scratch the soles of its feet without bending down.

I picked up an apple, calmly munching it while staring at the hole and one, two, three stones. My God! What on earth was that thing? Suddenly I was gripped by a sense of dread.

Tuesday 14 October 1958, *Le Pays d'Auge* newspaper

A Mystery Surrounds the Disappearance of Evelyne Parrot.

Madame Parrot, aged 39, married with no children, appears to have vanished into thin air on Friday 3rd October between Lisieux railway station and the home of her aunt Adèle in the rue de Rome in Paris. The matter is being investigated by the local police force in Lisieux, where she was last seen. All possibilities are being considered – an accident, kidnapping, a family drama, a Parisian vice ring.

Two witnesses have reported seeing Monsieur and Madame Parrot driving in their car towards Lisieux at about 9 a.m. The husband was dropping his wife off at the station, as he sometimes does. The same two witnesses confirmed seeing Julien Parrot drive back alone two hours later. Another witness, Madame Costet, who takes over milking the cows when Evelyne is away, said she heard the car engine making a spluttering noise before they set off. These reports are being followed up.

Sergeant Torus questioned Monsieur Parrot at his house, as well as the close family and friends. The couple has a good reputation, although some local people had been surprised to notice that Evelyne was more reserved than usual; according to the postman, she had been 'looking gloomy recently'. The enquiry is working on the theory that she disappeared somewhere in the vicinity of Saint-Lazare station in Paris. A ticket collector thinks he remembers seeing a dark-haired lady, who had bluish eyes and was smiling. A close inspection of the railtrack between Lisieux and Paris has not revealed anything.

When his wife did not come back on the 5 p.m. train on the 10th October and was not on the 8 p.m. one either, Monsieur Parrot alerted the police. Evelyne Parrot usually went to visit her aunt without arranging it with her in advance, since she had a set of keys to the flat. This means a week had elapsed before anyone realised she had disappeared, which makes the investigation more difficult. After a week, people cannot remember anything, or only hazily. The sergeant notes that there are many questions still unanswered.

This is the description of the woman who disappeared: she was just under five foot seven, had brown shoulder-length hair, blue eyes, a mole on her right cheek and an olive complexion. She was dressed in a beige suit, and was carrying a brown leather suitcase and a bright red shoulder bag. This is a photo of her. Anyone with any information is requested to contact the nearest police station.

From Part 2: A Whirlwind and Disunity Spring 1948

Monsieur Gifard gave his eldest daughter away in marriage in the spring. The wedding breakfast was held at the farm. The barn which housed the hay carts had been emptied for the occasion; branches of apple blossom and laurel decorated its walls. All the greenery adorning the place lent a feel of Christmas rather than Easter.

The snow-white tablecloths had been ironed immaculately, the chairs were arranged in perfectly straight lines as though for a military parade. The Ritz could not have done a finer job.

Rose, the bride-to-be, cut sheets of thick card into small squares, then she carefully traced all the letters in blue ink. It took a whole morning to sort out the seating plan, who should or should not sit next to whom, remembering not to put the cousins from Le Havre anywhere near those from Dozulé. There had been a quarrel over a cow and a bull which had been exchanged in order to give new blood to the herds. The male had died within two weeks during a coupling, which led to a feud; the relatives from Le Havre claimed those from Dozulé had overworked the well-endowed animal. The rest of the family turned it into a standing joke, alluding to Félix Faure, the French President who had died in the arms of his mistress. Rose spent a long while playing nervously with the labels bearing the names of the guests, shuffling them like a pack of cards. Evelyne and Julien ended up next to each other, and she murmured, 'Hmm, my second cousin who's so unwilling to think of getting married, why not?'

After the church service, the wedding feast began. Evelyne and Julien found themselves seated next to each other. He smiled, she scowled. She had sensed it was a trap, and was determined to keep her distance. To take her revenge, she began to talk to the cousin sitting opposite her. As she handed Julien the bread, the food and the water, she just said 'Here you are'. She thought he had been party to the plot. Julian ventured a few words at several points, but with no success.

As the afternoon wore on, Julien stood up and looking at the guests who had grown sleepy after all the drink and the copious food, he asked the world at large, 'How about going to see Louna's foal, it's two days old and as soft as a teddy bear!'

Suddenly Evelyne became like a child again. She seized Julien's hand and exclaimed, 'Oh, yes, let's all go!' And everyone else was caught up in her enthusiasm.

A happy band took the path through the woods towards the meadow, singing wedding songs. […]

Seven years later, 1958

The Parrots' daily life had taken on a regular rhythm over the years. Evelyne looked after the animals; they provided a channel for her maternal feelings. Her instinctive understanding of them impressed people. She could talk to them, take care of them and understand them.

Louna the mare, Frisette the donkey, Lark the cow who was leader of the herd, the duck called De Gaulle and the cockerel called Maurice Chevalier all respected their mistress and accorded her due deference. Evelyne stroked them, and handed out sugar lumps and dry bread. They would dig their muzzles or beaks into her pockets while Volga watched with displeasure. The dog was rather jealous and pushed aside any animal that took too long, even nipping the most persistent ones; she considered herself in charge of discipline in the household. Her guard duties were handsomely rewarded: every time she barked for a good reason, a square of chocolate was slipped into her mouth.

The farm had not purchased any new machinery since the time of the Parrots' wedding. A salesman had once turned up at the 'Lieu Malin' on a day when Evelyne was in a bad mood.

'Good day, Madam, could I speak to the owner?'

'You *are* speaking to the owner.'

'I'm selling tractors.'

'Fine, but we don't have the money at present.'

'But you would if you sold your horse to the butcher, and took out a little loan for the rest.'

'Well, I'll have a word with my horse, but if she doesn't like the idea it won't be easy to persuade her. Have you met my dog? She could see you back to your car, if you like. She gets a reward every time she does what she's asked to.'

Evelyne and Julien hadn't wanted to produce more milk or meat. Instead, they concentrated on their apples, and on the cider and especially the Calvados. Julien would deliver sacks of apples to people who liked to brew their daily alcohol, and he would also sell several tons to the cider press. The rest of the apples were secretly pressed in the hidden cellar. Just a small quantity of the Calvados was declared to the customs officials.

the babel anthology

Julien and Evelyne enjoyed this dangerous game. The illegal activity was exciting and frightening; after Lydia's death they craved this dizzying sensation, the stimulation of the forbidden. Volga would stand guard and warn them when anyone approached. They had made up a sign language, signalling with their hands like deaf people. A palm on top of a clenched fist meant 'Shh'.

Some local people who liked spirits would steal across the fields late in the evening, bringing rucksacks full of empty bottles. Sometimes they lit the alembic at night to make quite sure they were not discovered. As the alcohol dripped from the coils, it smelled like a real distillery.

Letter from Christina to Julien, Spring 1958

Dear Julien,

Thank you so much for your recent news. Your drawings are as good as ever. The portrait of your wife and the dog in front of your house are amazing.

Thomas and I separated in September. I did everything I could to keep our marriage together, but he came back from the Russian camps with memories which haunted him every night. His insomnia made him start drinking. On glass led to another until he became an alcoholic. He doesn't want to accept any treatment – brandy is his best friend, and the most deadly. He's killing himself. The doctor's said to me that unless he starts to talk about what he suffered, he'll just keep taking refuge in drink. In the Soviet Union, the regular German army had to support the SS. What did he do? What things did he witness? And then there were six years of enslavement under a communist regime, which broke him.

I found myself up against a brick wall, so I had to decide on a divorce. Lucas has been upset by the family break-up. He has a school teacher who spends his summer holidays from mid-July to mid-August near Caen, at Luc-sur-Mer. I think that's not far from where you live. Would you and Evelyne have my son to stay with you for a month over the summer? The change would do him so much good.

My best wishes to you both,

Christina

It was the afternoon of the 14th July, and the smell of haymaking wafted across the countryside. The sun and the slight breeze were drying the cut grass. The temperature was perfect for the hay, and the harvest gathered pace feverishly. Hay carts drove past each other on the way to the farms, horses winked at one another, farmers raised their caps and said, 'Hello,

Bernard, isn't this good weather, must make the most of it!'

There was a hum of activity. The village was like an anthill which had been suddenly kicked over. Everyone was animated; some had drunk too much because of the heat, some were afraid it would start to rain, others were excited by the women who took off layers of clothing because of the warm, inviting air.

Felicien Lecouec, the cockle and mussel seller, had turned up at the Parrots' gate in the morning. He had a bike, but used it to transport his gear rather than himself. A few years ago, one of his feet had been partly consumed by a combine harvester, and ever since his legs had been different lengths.

'Good morning! Who wants some of my cockles and mussels?' he would shout into the old funnel which he used as a loudspeaker.

Evelyne leapt at the chance. She was expecting the German visitors for supper, and thought they couldn't often have the chance to eat seafood, especially not cooked in best Normandy cream.

In the early evening, a vehicle ground to a halt on the gravel drive. A long, black car, twice the size of the Parrots' Renault 4CV, scared away the hens which had been dozing under the spreading branches of the chestnut tree. Four people got out of the Mercedes. Frau and Herr Rothman and their daughter Inge embraced the Parrots stiffly; Lukas kissed Evelyne and Julien.

The atmosphere soon became warmer and friendly. Over dinner, Julien spoke in German to Frau Rothman, while her husband translated for Evelyne, and the two children moved back and forth between French and German. Julien invited the guests to spend the night at the 'Lieu Malin'.

'You can't set off now, have our bedroom. Evelyne loves sleeping outside, the Milky Way makes her feel romantic.' Inge can share Lukas's room. How does that sound?'

'We'd be very pleased to accept, but on the condition that tomorrow you let us help you with the haymaking.'

They all got up slowly, trying to keep their balance, and went to bed in a haze of alcohol.

[...]

the babel anthology

from Part 3: **Giddy Memories Of The Past Late Summer 1939**

On the 2nd September 1939, father and son took their leave of each other, with tears in their eyes. Paternal injunctions echoed in Julien's ears as he set off:

'Watch out for mustard gas, they're bound to have kept some, damned Germans.'

'Yes, Dad. You take care of yourself.'

For eight months the strange war sapped the soldiers' spirits. Their nerves were on edge from the lack of action; the more optimistic among them just wanted it to end. To pass the time, Julien would draw portraits in his little sketchbook, and sometimes he sold his work to his comrades.

On the 10th May 1940, the German offensive struck, with a lightning war against the Netherlands, Belgium and Luxembourg. While the French army went to the aid of Belgium, German tanks crossed the Ardennes, then broke through the front lines at Sedan. Julien found himself at Loon, near Dunkirk, caught in a whirlwind of death. He was stranded on the beach, harassed by the Stuka pilots; machine guns and tanks appeared at the top of the dunes. Trapped by the sea, like many of his comrades, he surrendered.

This was the start of their captivity, an enormous crowd of men, stunned by the rapidity of their defeat.

Under the watchful gaze of the guards, the prisoners had to march fifteen miles a day in the direction of Germany.

Julien planned to escape at the first opportunity, and meanwhile he tried to make sense of a few of the foreign words. There was a man from Alsace in his group who acted as translator, and Julien noted down the most useful phrases in his notebook.

The prisoners' main preoccupation was getting fresh water. The thin soup bothered their stomachs, and many men started to feel permanently dizzy from lack of sustenance. At night, the defeated men were parked in huge fields, closely guarded by the enemy. They had to sleep on the earth, there were no toilets, and they had nothing to keep them occupied.

One morning, two corpses riddled with gunshot wounds were dragged in front of the prisoners. They were told that they could try to escape if they wanted, but they would be choosing death.

After the forced march, his feet bleeding, Julien ended up at POW Camp Number Six in Hammersdorf. He was first sent to work in an armament factory; the heat of the foundry was unbearable. When the metal had been poured into a mould, it had to be cooled with water. Julien spent his days in a muggy 90 degrees. The pounds fell off his body, although fortunately some food parcels arrived from France.

One day at roll-call he was told to move to another line. The authorities now sent him to the railway track to replace sleepers and rails. The work was equally hard here, but there was a real sense of camaraderie, whereas in the factory the humidity and the high temperatures had mentally drained the workers and made them apathetic. On the railway, the men stuck together and tried to win small victories over the Germans. When they had to lift a heavy load, they made sure the weakest men were in the middle of the chain. Sometimes they even went in for a little sabotage, messing up screws so that jobs took longer and they could have a break, or burying wood screws in the scree.

Meanwhile, Julien continued to learn more German.

The carnage at Stalingrad at the end of 1942 meant that all German men were called back up for active service, even those who had previously been declared unfit or too old. As a result, the German countryside was left without farm workers.

Since the invasion of Belgium, Christina had been running her farm on her own, employing two men, but now these workers were replaced by four skeletal prisoners, Julien, Michel, Jacques and Jojo. She had told the commander of the prison camp that she would rather have French prisoners: 'I speak the language, so it will be easier for me to give them orders.' The non-commissioned officer had agreed to the request, saying, 'Anyway, the Führer said we've got to make sure the Poles and the Russians get the roughest jobs.' Julien was put in charge of the foursome. 'If one of you escapes, you'll end up in front of a military tribunal,' barked the officer.

Frau Christina Brüner met the four men in her paved courtyard. In good French, she gave them instructions, told them the timetable and the daily tasks allotted to them; there were fifteen cows to take care of and twenty-five acres of potatoes to farm. She finished by saying, 'If you work well, I'll feed you better than the camp does. Would you like a mug of coffee?' In the middle of the morning, Frau Brüner gave the prisoners a hot drink and slices of bread spread with butter; at mid-day there was a proper meal, often potatoes with a little meat. She knew that men can't work on an empty stomach.

Very quickly Christina and Julien struck up a friendship. From the beginning, there was something between them, perhaps a mutual recognition of what they shared in this world where everyone was struggling to survive. She realised that she could count on his discretion, and she could be open with him. She already spoke French, he was trying to learn her language. It soon became a game. At breakfast, she would talk to him slowly in German. One day, when the other three prisoners had been sent to clear snow in the village, she told him a little about her life. In 1934 she had been teaching French in the neighbouring village. The Nazis had accused her of failing to denounce two Jewish girls in her class, and as a result she had been forced to return to helping her husband Thomas on the farm.

'Strange things happen in the war. I've been given another chance to speak your language, Julien. But why do you want to learn ours?'

'I'd like to escape.'

'Shh, don't be stupid. I'm a spy.'

'All prisoners want to. But since I've been at this farm, I feel as though there's hope again, it's given me a new lease of life.'

[...]

charles baudelaire
beginning and end

'Le Poète est semblable au prince des nuées
Qui hante la tempête et se rit de l'archer;
Exilé sur le sol au milieu des huées,
Ses ailes de géant l'empêchent de marcher'

A dusty little-used room at the editor's school was 'The French Library' and there an unwary youngster picked up the soft yellow-covered volume of *Les Fleurs du Mal* in the *Pléiade* edition (that's to say with all the previously censored material diligently put back in). With a few leafings the great poet inducted him into the legion of the 'perverse'; experimenters with experience, sensation and sensuality. Under the school uniform of dreary imperial serge and flannel a new and stranger being was born... *Je te remercie très bien Charles, vive la France! Vive la culture française! Liberté, Egalité, Perversité!*

So as part of our launch issue's tribute to France and to C. B. we include his '*L'Albatros*' in the original with Merryn Williams' translation. M.W. has published three collections of poetry and is a former editor of *The Interpreter's House*. She attended *tba*'s pre-launch reading at the Jam Factory in Oxford, a place – paradoxically – once famous for marmalade. Nowadays they serve good beer, have clean toilets and a special room for literary events. All Hail the Jammers!

charles baudelaire
the albatross

Translated by Merryn Williams

Often, to pass the time, a crew will catch
an albatross, that great bird of the sea
who trails a ship for weeks and months across
the bitter waters, flapping lazily.

Immediately they've got him on the deck,
this king of blue – who just now used to soar
so gracefully – allows his wings to sag -
pathetic! – as a tired man drags an oar.

That winged white bird, how clumsy and how weak!
An ugly object now, and put to shame.
So, one man sticks a pipe into his beak;
one mimics him, pretending to be lame.

He's like a poet. The majestic bird
who rides the storm, defies the men who stalk
him with their arrows – crashes to the ground,
is mocked. His giant wings won't let him walk.

charles baudelaire
l'albatros

Souvent, pour s'amuser, les hommes d'équipage
Prennent des albatros, vastes oiseaux des mers,
Qui suivent, indolents compagnons de voyage,
Le navire glissant sur les gouffres amers.

À peine les ont-ils déposés sur les planches,
Que ces rois de l'azur, maladroits et honteux,
Laissent piteusement leurs grandes ailes blanches
Comme des avirons traîner à côté d'eux.

Ce voyageur ailé, comme il est gauche et veule!
Lui, naguère si beau, qu'il est comique et laid!
L'un agace son bec avec un brûle-gueule,
L'autre mime, en boitant, l'infirme qui volait!

Le Poète est semblable au prince des nuées
Qui hante la tempête et se rit de l'archer;
Exilé sur le sol au milieu des huées,
Ses ailes de géant l'empêchent de marcher

the babel anthology

next issues

The next *tba* will be new english writing + *l'avventura italiana* including writing (in English translation) by Dolores Prato, Paolo Cognetti, Adrian Bravi, Francesca Scotti, Giuseppe Munforte, Fulvio Ervas, Carola Susani, Laura Fidaleo, Antonella Moscati and Felice Cimatti.

tba3 will be new english writing + *Brazilian Outsiders* including writing (in English translation) by Bernardo Kucinski et al.

subscriptions

tba is a book anthology series, appears twice a year and is available in bookshops or online.

Direct from the publisher only, the subscription price is £6 per issue + £2 post and packing (UK), £3 (Europe) £5 (rest of world). State which issues you already have and don't wish duplicated. In **epub, mobi** or **pdf** format same price but without postage charge.

subscriptions offers

'*early adopters*': give *tba* a good start in life: be one of the first 250 to subscribe but act quickly for this deal!

1 year/2 issues: £10 + postage + free book*

2 years/4 issues £18 + postage + 2 free books*

payment

For the special direct subscription price we need to minimise costs so only paypal payment or UK cheque is accepted. Cheques to 'Boulevard Books' posted to Boulevard, 71 Lytton Road, Oxford OX4 3NY

Paypal, open your paypal account and send relevant sum to ray.keenoy@ gmail.com, making sure you have given us your address and telling us any issues you don't want.

*free books, choose when you order, no extra postage

Sandra Petrignani *The Toy Catalogue*

Caio Fernando Abreu *Dragons...* (warning, explicit content)

Babel Guide to Scandinavian Fiction in Translation

Babel Guide to German Fiction in Translation

submissions

Two editions of *tba* are published every year and we seek contemporary writing in English, max 5000 words, but preferably less, from authors, agents and publishers for this high-quality showcase for their work. We also aim to reprint contemporary pieces from literary magazines, small press work etc, hopefully giving it a wider window and a more permanent and accessible form

As of March 2013 *tba* is financed from sales and sweat only so we cannot offer fees to authors or translators.

We also seek foreign language pieces, either new translations of 'out-of-copyright' classics or previously untranslated works, please also see 'Collaborators'.

Please send submissions by email to info@babelguides.co.uk. Do not send anything over 5000 words. For longer pieces, novel extracts etc, please send one or two selections made by you that are reasonably stand-alone.

collaborators

We seek guest editors for our language sections who would be able to contact and invite foreign publishers to send extracts or short pieces representing their authors for subsequent editions. Small fee offered for guest editors. In general we are looking for work not previously translated and published in the UK.

interns etc

Editorial, layout, marketing and fund-raising volunteers/interns. If you have or perhaps wish to gain experience in these areas please get in touch telling us something about yourself, your skills and interests. We can work locally with people in Oxford, London or Tuscany or anywhere remotely with skype and email.

rate card

B/W advertising pages in *tba* cost £100 + VAT.

Half and quarter pages *pro rata*.

Size: w138mm by h215mm

Artwork to: info@babelguides.co.uk

multi-buy

We hope you've enjoyed reading *tba* and can see its potential both as a conduit for new writing in English and for bringing fresh world writing into the literary diet of English-speakers. Though we wouldn't say no to stuffed brown envelopes, a way to push the anthology series is to take extra copies to give as presents or to sell to others who might be interested. Our special rate for this is £4 for subscribers or contributors. Please add 15% for postage.

mate watch

If you're reading this you probably know 5 or 10 or more people who would enjoy *tba* and support what it's doing. Rather than complaining about how Amazon is decimating publishing or how globalisation is killing off national literature (they are) act as an involved citizen by aiding an initiative to widen the circle of literature and reading. Either give or send a friend a copy of *tba* or contact us for a friendly publicity email or weblink so others can learn about *tba* and see samples of our content. You forward the email with your comment; we will only have their email address if they subsequently contact us themselves. If you are in touch with any authors or translators, potential language or guest editors then please do the same. A few minutes of your time could win us a new subscriber and grow the project and the space it provides outside corporate publishing.

website

thebabelanthology.com

World Literature in English translation – a unique resource: the 'Babel Guides' series from Boulevard

'both hip and useful' *The Guardian*

'a brillliant idea well executed' *The Good Book Guide*

Babel Guide to Dutch and Flemish Fiction in Translation

978 1899460802 £12.95

Babel Guide to Welsh Fiction 978 1899460519 £14.95

Babel Guide to Brazilian Fiction in Translation

978 1899460700 £12.95

Babel Guide to Hungarian Fiction in Translation

978 1899460854 £12.95

Babel Guide to Italian Fiction in Translation

978 1899460007 £7.95

Babel Guide to the Fiction of Portugal, Brazil and Africa in Translation

978 18994600052 £7.95

Babel Guide to German Fiction in Translation

978 1899460209 £9.95

Babel Guide to French Fiction in Translation

978 1899460101 £9.95

Babel Guide to Jewish Fiction in Translation

978 1899460250 £9.95

Babel Guide to Scandinavian Fiction in Translation

978 1899460304 £9.95

Babel Guide to South Indian Fiction

978 1899460564 £9.95

Available in bookshops or see babelguides.co.uk (also epub/pdf)

Boulevard Books are distributed in the UK by:

Gazelle, White Cross Mills, Lancaster, LA1 4XS +44(0)152468765
www.gazellebooks.co.uk

Real food:
from the farm to your plate

Fresh fruit & vegetables from local farmers

Local organic farmers harvest the season's best produce from their fields...

The VegVan
Mobile Greengrocer's Shop

You take it home in your shopping bag every week at our stops around Oxford

Easy!

www.cultivateoxford.org

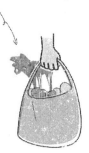

ⒷZ editions

www.cbeditions.com

'the idiosyncratic genius of
CB editions'
– Nicholas Lezard, *Guardian*

Founded in 2007, CB editions
publishes short fiction and
poetry, including work in
translation, and runs the annual
Free Verse Poetry Book Fair
(www.poetrybookfair.com).

Fergus Allen
Apollinaire
Jonathan Barrow
Beverley Bie Brahic
Andrzej Bursa
Andrew Elliott
Nancy Gaffield
Joaquin Giannuzzi
Stefan Grabinski
Gert Hofmann
Gabriel Josipovici
Stephen Knight
Tony Lurcock
Todd McEwen
David Markson
Miha Mazzini
J. O. Morgan
D. Nurkse
Francis Ponge
Jack Robinson
Dai Vaughan

'the admirable CB editions' – Boyd Tonkin, *Independent* / 'the enterprising CB editions'
– Geoff Dyer, *Guardian* / 'the enterprising CB editions' – Ben Wilkinson, *Times Literary Supplement* / 'the estimable CB editions' – Dai George, *Poetry Review* / 'dedicated to publishing surprising books' – *Sunday Times* / 'the one-man wonder that is CB editions' – John Self, *Asylum* / 'the wonderfully eclectic, quietly iconoclastic CBe' – Mike Loveday, *Eyewear* / 'the consistently amazing CB editions – Robin Boothroyd, *The Cold Tap Sings* / 'one of the most original and enterprising of the small presses' – Nicholas Murray, *Guardian* / 'the admirably wayward CB editions' – Jeremy Noel-Tod, *The Lyre*

the Albion BEatNiK
bookstore

34, Walton Street, Oxford, OX2 6AA
albionbeatnik @ yahoo.co.uk :: www.*albionbeatnikbooks*.co.uk

NEW & SECOND-HAND BOOKS

* * *

TERms $ DefiNitions :: BIBLIOPOLE is a book dealer

BIBLIOTAPH is somebody who hides or hoards books, possibly under lock and key

BIBLIOCLAST destroys books, for ideological reasons or not

BIBLIOPHILE is a collector of books and treasures them for

their value, beauty or content

A BIBLIOMANIAC is NUTS   [see left]

BIBLIOBONKERS is a more extreme version

BIBLIOPOLY booksElling by largE gl0BaL chains (or/ famous board gamE basEd on the book tradE)

ALBION is an old word for England   ://:

BEATNIK is an American slang word for AN ATTITUDE OF
MIND, introduced by Jack Kerouac in 1948 (he claimed from the word 'beatific')

BOOKWORMS are always reading books, or are the larvae of various insects, moths and beetles that live in and feed upon the pages of books. [No single species can properly be called the bookworm.] Central heating, the manufacturing materials of modern books, the poor state of the English language as is writ today, and the prevailing attention span of gnats, have curtailed their medieval activities. **BUCK THE TREND !!**